# ASSET PROTECTION
# 101

## BOOKS IN THE TRUMP UNIVERSITY SERIES

# TRUMP
## UNIVERSITY

# ASSET PROTECTION 101

**Tax and
Legal Strategies
of the Rich**

J. J. CHILDERS

John Wiley & Sons, Inc.

Published by John Wiley & Sons, Inc., Hoboken, New Jersey.
Published simultaneously in Canada.

Wiley Bicentennial Logo: Richard J. Pacifico

For general information on our other products and services or for technical support, please contact our Customer Care Department within the United States at (800) 762-2974, outside the United States at (317) 572-3993 or fax (317) 572-4002.

Wiley also publishes its books in a variety of electronic formats. Some content that appears in print may not be available in electronic books. For more information about Wiley products, visit our web site at www.wiley.com.

***Library of Congress Cataloging-in-Publication Data***

Childers, J. J.
    Trump University asset protection 101 : tax and legal strategies of the rich / J. J. Childers.
      p. cm.
    "Published simultaneously in Canada."
    ISBN 978-0-470-17464-7 (cloth)
      1. Tax planning—United States—Popular works. 2. Tax consultants—United States—Popular works. 3. Liability (Law)—United States—Popular works. 4. Estate planning—United States—Popular works. I. Trump University. II. Title. III. Title: Asset protection 101. IV. Title: Asset protection one hundred one. V. Title: Asset protection one hundred and one.
  KF6297.Z9C589 2008
  343.7305'23—dc22

                                                2007033357

Printed in the United States of America.

10  9  8  7  6  5  4  3  2  1

*To my wife Jill and my daughters, Mary Katherine and Annabelle, my inspiration and my greatest supporters.*

# CONTENTS

# CONTENTS

# CONTENTS

# FOREWORD TO THE TRUMP UNIVERSITY 101 SERIES

People often ask me the secret to my success, and the answer is simple: focus, hard work, and tenacity. I've had some lucky breaks, but luck will only get you so far. You also need business savvy—not necessarily a degree from Wharton, but you do need the desire and discipline to educate yourself. I created Trump University to give motivated businesspeople the skills required to achieve lasting success.

The *Trump University 101 Series* explains the most powerful and important ideas in business—the same concepts taught in the most respected MBA curriculums and used by the most successful companies in the world, including The Trump Organization. Each book is written by a top professor, author, or entrepreneur, whose goal is to help you put these ideas to use in your business right away. If you're not satisfied with the status quo in your career, read this book, pick one key idea, and implement it. I guarantee it will make you money.

DONALD J. TRUMP

# ACKNOWLEDGMENTS

Writing a book is one of the most challenging endeavors one could tackle. A lot of work goes into completing a large number of components in order to pull it off. There is no way that I could do it without the assistance and teamwork of some great people.

First and foremost I'd like to thank Donald J. Trump and all of the great folks at Trump University for providing me with this tremendous opportunity. Michael Sexton, David Highbloom, and the rest of the team there have put together something really special that I am proud to be a part of. Richard Narramore, Senior Editor at Wiley & Sons, was a tremendous help in putting together the concept and flow for the book and making it a reality. I'm indebted to my friends and agents, Mark Dove and Ragnar Danneskjold, for the work that they do in making things happen.

My book writing team really made things possible and this book would not be complete without their tireless efforts. Attorney D. Bryce Finley made a major impact with his assembly and review of the legal concepts contained throughout the book. Tax attorney Craig S. Lair provided great input and insight into retirement plans and how to gain control through self-direction. My friend and personal tax CPA Johnny Tollett played an integral part in the project with his tax knowledge and illustrations. He has been a key factor in the success of this book as well as all of the other products and services that we are able to provide.

My long-time friend and assistant Michele Hunter did an amazing job in putting things together and coordinating all of our efforts. Without the assistance of these professionals, this book would not be in existence.

My favorite CPA, my wife Jill Childers, provided great assistance in proofreading and making sure that things were assembled in a way that made sense. This, on top of the patience and understanding that she exhibits in putting up with my work schedule, made things much easier and enables me to do everything I do.

I'd also like to thank my parents, John and Brenda Childers, for teaching me the importance and power of financial education. Growing up in an entrepreneurial environment and witnessing the attitudes necessary to make all things possible provided invaluable training that has reaped enormous rewards.

Finally, I'd like to thank all those believers in the American Dream. Small business owners, entrepreneurs, and capitalists are what keep the engine running. If this book helps them to keep more of their hard-earned money, my work has made the impact I've intended.

# I

---

TAX SECRETS OF THE
WEALTHY

# 1

## WHY MAKING MONEY IS NOT ENOUGH

### *The Closely Guarded Secret of the Wealthy*

When I set out to write this book, some people believed it would only appeal to a small percentage of the population since it dealt with protecting wealth rather than creating wealth. The idea that wealth protection is only important for an exclusive group is actually a common misconception that keeps our nation's wealth out of the hands of many and in the hands of a select few. What most people fail to realize is that the *protection* of wealth goes hand in hand with the *creation* of wealth. In fact, *wealth protection* is an essential step for anyone seeking to create and build lasting wealth. Wealthy families know this. They understand asset protection is the primary tool for safeguarding their assets so that they can continue to become wealthier. This book is not only for those who have already built a sizable financial portfolio but also for those seeking to do so.

The topic of asset protection is amazing, cunning, baffling, powerful, and tricky. For some, it means nothing more than making sure that they hold on to the money they currently possess. For others, it's an area reserved only for those "rare" individuals who might find themselves on the receiving end of a lawsuit. Others believe (mistakenly) that it's something someone else needs to worry about. The truth is that asset protection is the closely guarded secret of the wealthy that enables them to build and grow their wealth on an ongoing basis. This book shows you how to tap into the financial secrets that the wealthy (and their advisors, like me) know about. Asset protection is the foundation of all wealth building; you must understand it if you are ever to join the ranks of the financial elite.

## Key to Financial Independence

Most people think that the key to financial independence is to simply increase their income. While this is important, making more money, in and of itself, will not make you wealthy. The only way to become wealthy is to continually increase the gap between the amount of money that comes in and the amount that goes out. That's it.

When I was growing up, my dad was a successful real estate investor, developer, and entrepreneur. One of his business endeavors was to travel the country teaching people to build wealth through the vehicle of real estate. I remember telling my dad that someday I wanted to make a lot of money like him. I still remember his response. He said, "Son, making money is important, but *building wealth* is more important." I wasn't sure what he meant at the time, but as I worked with literally thousands of clients over the years, his words began to make a lot of sense. I've seen far too many people who have made a lot of money but weren't able to keep enough to ever become wealthy. Even if they did keep a sizeable portion of their money, they often lost it all through taxes, lawsuits, and other misfortunes. You see, regardless of how much income you generate, you'll never become a millionaire unless you *accumulate* a million dollars worth of assets over and above your liabilities. Simply put, *you have to keep more of what you make*. That's what asset protection is all about.

## Government Sponsored Attack on Wealth

Most people don't recognize the threats to their keeping their money. In fact, they rely on others for their protection rather than taking control of their assets. Many people even look to the government for protection—like sheep hoping the wolf will protect them. My practice and businesses are dedicated to helping individuals identify the potential threats to their wealth and then formulating and implementing a plan for protecting their hard-earned assets. This book explains what you're up against in your quest to become (or stay) wealthy.

While the masses lean on the government for their protection, the wealthy understand that the government has a very sophisticated strategy for extracting wealth from its citizens. State and federal governments, along with other sources, are attempting to place what I refer to as a LID on wealth. LID is an acronym for the three major threats to wealth: (1) Lawsuits, (2) Income taxes, and (3) Death taxes. To become wealthy, you must blow this LID off your business and personal financial situation.

This book helps you create a security system to protect your assets. It's organized around three key topics:

1. Tax reduction.
2. Protection from lawsuits.
3. Estate and retirement planning.

Let's take a brief look at each of these.

## Tax Reduction: Legal Ways to Downsize Uncle Sam

The biggest ongoing threat to your wealth is the income tax. At the asset protection and tax seminars that I conduct throughout the country, I often ask, "What is the single biggest expense that you incur each and every year?" Surprisingly enough, few people realize that the biggest expense, even bigger than their mortgage in most instances, comes in the form of taxes. Even worse, most people fail to realize that there is actually something they can do to avoid many of the taxes they pay. If you plan on becoming (or staying) wealthy, you must learn to *legally* combat your tax bill.

As an attorney who specializes in tax reduction, I hear people complain about their taxes all the time. I always ask them the same question: *What are you doing about it?* The blank look on the faces of these people shows me that they believe that tax reduction is an oxymoron. Many people don't believe it's possible. For the rich, however, tax reduction is a daily reality that enables them to spend before-tax dollars while others pay for items with after-tax dollars. If you don't understand what I mean by that, keep reading.

The simple fact is that nobody cares about reducing your taxes more than you do. Since that's the case, you must learn how to do it—and it will make a tremendous difference in your financial life. The strategies in this book enable you to follow in their steps to install your very own asset security system against taxes, as well as lawsuits and death taxes.

## Protection from Lawsuits: Escaping Lawsuit Hell

When it comes to lawsuits, most people have heard horror stories of individuals who have been sued for ridiculous things, things that are often out of their control. A cover story in *Newsweek* magazine described our situation as "Lawsuit Hell." Studies show that a new lawsuit is filed in this country every 30 seconds on average. In the short time that it's taken you to read this chapter, several lawsuits have already been filed somewhere against somebody. Lives have been changed, forever. Financial pictures have been altered, irrevocably. Entire family futures have been put in jeopardy. The worst part is that these lawsuits often could have been avoided with a few simple preventative measures. You will learn more about this in later chapters.

## Estate and Retirement Planning: Avoiding the Wealth Death Penalty

Wealth death penalty refers to the estate taxes imposed on those who build up appreciable amounts of wealth. If you die leaving no assets for your heirs and beneficiaries, the government is not concerned. However, if you actually accumulate some wealth to pass on to your loved ones, the government feels the need to penalize you. While this may not make sense, this is exactly how the system works. The government does this through the implementation of death taxes.

Most people spend more time planning their vacations than they do their estates. Studies have indicated that the average person will spend over 90 thousand hours working to accumulate wealth (40 hours a week times 50 weeks a year for 45 years of their working lives), but less than 3 hours learning how to preserve that wealth. Most people fail to plan their estates—and their families unexpectedly discover that the wealth their loved one spent a lifetime building is largely consumed by estate taxes, fees, and other expenses. Many of these situations could have been avoided by implementing simple estate plans using the tools you will be learning as you read this book. Wealthy families in this country take estate planning seriously because they know how bad government intervention can be. You must adopt this mentality.

*Unlocking Einstein's Most Powerful Force*   Retirement is the light at the end of the tunnel that makes some of the dark times of our working lives more tolerable. Unfortunately, a large majority of workers will never experience the type of retirement that they dream of.

Why is this? Primarily because they don't understand what Albert Einstein called the most powerful force on earth: *compounding growth*. Today most people have access to something even more powerful, *tax-sheltered compound growth*, through their company-sponsored or self-established retirement plans. With this type of millionaire-making mechanism available, it would seem like a no-brainer that most of us would invest in it. But in practice, few people have any sort of savings plan to provide for themselves and their families when their working days are over. To make things worse, people live much longer today than in previous decades. You can see the type of crisis that awaits our society if people don't begin to make a change.

The chapters in this book on retirement planning will get you well on your way to building wealth through the power of tax-sheltered compounding growth. You will see how to personally take control over your retirement plans to turbo-charge the power of your pensions and reap enormous returns.

## Asset-Sheltering Legal Entities of the Rich

Most people don't realize that there are legal entities they could be using right now which would:

1.  Reduce their tax liability by 30 percent, 40 percent, even 50 percent.
2.  Avoid liability associated with frivolous lawsuits.
3.  Pass on literally millions of dollars to their heirs estate tax-free.
4.  Build wealth faster by keeping more of their profits.

Implementing an *Asset Security System* is the process of blending various legal entities in a way that maximizes the advantages of each entity while minimizing any potential disadvantages. My practice uses a customized approach that is different from other types of asset protection programs because it is not a one-size-fits-all plan. This book helps you design a plan that fits your individual situation. It is the key component in helping you effectively manage your personal financial situation and begin keeping more of your hard-earned assets to build wealth.

# 2

---

# CRACKING THE TAX CODE

## *How Understanding Different Types of Taxes, Income, and Taxpayers Can Significantly Reduce and Even Eliminate Taxes*

> I shall never use profanity except in discussing
> house rent and taxes.
>
> MARK TWAIN

Why would someone willingly pay more in taxes than the law requires if they don't have to? The answer is simple. These people fall into two key categories:

1. Lack of knowledge.
2. Lack of effort.

Let's talk about the second one first. Plain and simple, these people just aren't willing to do what it takes to reduce their tax bill. A large reason for this is that they are afraid of being audited by the Internal Revenue Service (IRS). Many people are so frightened of the process and the potential penalties involved in making mistakes that they make themselves sick when thinking about it all. If that sounds like you, here's comedian Jay Leno's advice:

> Worried about an IRS audit? Avoid what's called a red flag. That's something the IRS always looks for. For example, say you have some money left in your bank account after paying taxes. That's a red flag.

The fact is, you don't have to be scared of the IRS. Americans have every right—some would say a duty—to pay as little tax as legally possible. Speaking for the Supreme Court, Justice George Sutherland wrote:

> The legal right of a taxpayer to decrease the amount of what otherwise would be his taxes, or altogether avoid them, by means which the law permits, cannot be doubted. (Gregory v. Helvering, 293 U.S. 465; 55 S. Ct. 266; 79 L. Ed. 596)

The reason most people pay too much in taxes is not necessarily lack of effort or fear of the IRS but lack of knowledge. They have never had someone explain to them in simple terms how the tax system works and what they can do to keep more—much more—of their hard-earned money. This chapter explains the basic types of taxes you have to first understand before you can make a tax reduction plan that will substantially increase your long-term wealth.

## Types of Taxes: Understanding What You're Up Against

Many of us spend more on taxes each year than on food, clothing, and shelter combined. Yet, amazingly, we really don't know much about taxes. If you've received a paycheck, you know that your employer holds taxes out of your pay. But my guess is that you don't know exactly what types of taxes are held out and at what rates. The amounts are huge, but we focus only on our "net" income. I've often said that if we wanted true tax reform in America, we would do away with employer withholdings and make *every* taxpayer actually write a check to Uncle

Sam for what normally comes out of their checks. Try signing that check every week and now see how excited you are to reduce your tax bill.

If you analyze the taxes that come out of your check, you will generally see four types of withholdings:

1. Federal income tax.
2. Social Security.
3. Medicare.
4. State income tax.

In some states, there are additional taxes that are withheld, but for the purposes of this chapter, we will focus on these four.

Federal income taxes are withheld based on how you fill out the W-4 form you receive from your employer. Current federal individual tax rates range from zero percent all the way up to 35 percent. The factors that determine your personal tax rate are your marital status, number of dependents, and itemized deductions including mortgage interest, state and local taxes, and charitable contributions.

Social Security tax is currently held out of your paycheck at the rate of 6.2 percent on your first $97,500 in wages. So, for the majority of taxpayers, the full amount (6.2 percent) of Social Security tax is withheld. Your employer has the obligation to match this amount dollar-for-dollar. You pay 6.2 percent. Your employer pays 6.2 percent. Combined, that is 12.4 percent. If you happen to own your own business, you are both the employee and the employer. Therefore, you must pay 12.4 percent in Social Security tax *before* you pay a dime in income tax.

On top of this, Medicare tax is currently held out of your paycheck at the rate of 1.45 percent. Unlike Social Security tax, Medicare tax is not capped at a certain earnings threshold. Every dollar you earn is subject to Medicare tax. Your employer is required to match these taxes as well. Therefore, self-employed individuals must pay 2.9 percent of Medicare tax on their entire earnings. Once again, this is *before* paying the first dime in income tax.

The combination of Social Security and Medicare tax, or Federal Insurance Contributions Act (FICA), is 7.65 percent for the individual and 7.65 percent for the employer. Combined, that equates to a tax of 15.3 percent for self-employed individuals. This is referred to as the self-employment tax.

Many of you reading this book are looking for new ways to bring in income and build wealth. Often you will begin this process while maintaining your full-time job in order to keep your personal cash flow intact until such a time as your new business can support your lifestyle. Let's assume for the moment that you are in the 25 percent tax bracket (where most working Americans end up) and you have started your own business to supplement your employment. Your self-employed earnings will *start* being taxed at a federal rate of 25 percent because that is where your other earnings and deductions have left you. Add to that the 15.3 percent self-employment tax on your business earnings and you are now paying 40.3 percent. Depending on what state you live in, you may have additional income tax to pay. You see, it doesn't take long at all before taxes are climbing close to 50 percent of your income. The worst part about it is that you are really not making a lot of money if you are in the 25 percent federal income tax bracket.

Of course, simply gaining a working knowledge of taxes withheld from your paycheck will not solve your problem. However, becoming aware of the situation enables us to begin to address this problem.

## What You Don't Know *Can* Hurt You

Not all income is taxed equally. To illustrate, here's an example.

*Tax Structuring with Barney and Betty*

*Example 1*
**Facts:**

Barney and Betty are married and combined make $70,000 in wages.

Their itemized deductions and personal exemptions equal $20,000.

They live in a state with a 7 percent income tax rate.

| | | |
|---|---|---|
| Federal Income Tax | $6,800.00 | |
| State Income Tax | $3,500.00 | |
| Social Security and Medicare | $5,355.00 | |
| Tax Burden | $15,655.00 | 22 percent |

*Example 2*
**Facts:**

Barney is employed by an excavating company and earns $55,000 per year.

Betty is employed as a fashion designer and earns $60,000 per year.

Their itemized deductions and personal exemptions equal $30,000.

They live in a state with a 7 percent income tax rate.

| | | |
|---|---|---|
| Federal Income Tax | $14,870.00 | |
| State Income Tax | $5,950.00 | |
| Social Security and Medicare | $8,798.00 | |
| Tax Burden | $29,618.00 | 26 percent |

*Example 3*
**Facts:**

Barney is self-employed by an excavating company and nets $55,000 per year.

Betty is self-employed as a fashion designer and earns $60,000 per year.

Their itemized deductions and personal exemptions equal $30,000.

They live in a state with a 7 percent income tax rate

| Federal Income Tax | $12,839.00 | |
| State Income Tax | $5,950.00 | |
| Social Security and Medicare | $16,249.00 | |
| Tax Burden | $35,038.00 | 30 percent |

*Example 4*
**Facts:**

Barney leases an office building to an excavating company and has a taxable net of $55,000.

Betty invests in real estate and earned $60,000 in capital gains.

Their itemized deductions and personal exemptions equal $30,000.

They live in a state with a 7 percent income tax rate

| Federal Income Tax | $8,875.00 | |
| State Income Tax | $5,950.00 | |
| Social Security and Medicare | $0.00 | |
| Tax Burden | $14,825.00 | 13 percent |

If you study the examples closely, you will see some alarming numbers. Income in Example 2 went up 64 percent, however, actual tax dollars went up 89 percent. That math just doesn't add up. Example 3 contains the same amount of income as Example 2, however, the total dollars paid in taxes is substantially more. Did you notice that less total tax is paid in Example 4 than Example 1 even though income is significantly higher? The reason for these variances is that different types of income are subject to paying different types of tax. As you can see, obtaining knowledge of different types of income can go a long way in stretching the family budget. Because that is the case, we need to get a better understanding of these different types.

*Different Types of Income*

*Earned income* is income that you earn for your personal services. Earned income is subject to both income tax and self-employment tax

(Social Security and Medicare). The most common type of earned income is W-2 wages (salary, etc.). Net income from a self-employed business (filed on Schedule C) is also considered earned income. This is the type of income we want to minimize or avoid if possible because it is taxed most heavily.

*Passive income* is income that is generated from something other than personal services. Passive income is subject to income tax, but is not subject to self-employment tax. The most common type of passive income is rental property. You see, the income you generate from rental property is not based on your personal services, but rather on the value of your property and the rental income that it generates. Passive income can also be generated by your personal involvement, or lack thereof, in your business. Certain business entities such as limited partnerships can create passive income. We'll talk more about these later when we review the different types of taxpayers.

*Portfolio income* is income you earn on your investments. This type of income includes interest, dividends, and capital gains. It is subject to income tax, but not self-employment tax. In this way, portfolio income is very similar to passive income. One major difference between the two is the ability to pay even less tax by generating capital gains. Currently, capital gains are taxed at a maximum rate of 15 percent. That's right, a maximum of 15 percent. It is highly likely that this historically low rate will not be around forever. Therefore, it would be a very wise move to analyze your investments to see if there is a way to maximize your overall return by taking advantage of this tremendous tax break while it exists.

*Deferred income* is income that you do not pay tax on currently, but that you expect to pay tax on at some point in the future. That tax could be paid next year, 10 years from now, at retirement, or possibly never. Retirement plans are an easy way to set up deferred income. The way that it works is you take a current deduction today for the amount you contribute to your retirement plan. You will most likely pay tax when that money is removed from your retirement plan. However, that time will hopefully be many years from now when you may be in a lower tax bracket than you are currently. Section 1031, or like-kind, exchanges are another way to generate tax-deferred income for real estate properties. In this scenario, you can sell a piece of property at a gain and defer the tax on that gain by acquiring another investment property. There are certain parameters you have to meet, but tax-savvy investors would be wise to know all the ins and outs of Section 1031 exchanges.

*Tax-free income* is exactly that, wonderfully tax free. The primary tax-free income bonanza for most working Americans is experienced on the sale of their personal residence. If you use a home as your main, or principal, residence for any two out of the preceding five years, any gain on the sale of that home would be tax-free up to the first $250,000 of gain for a single filer or $500,000 for married filers.

Often, investments that yield tax-free income, even though the returns may be lower, will have an effective rate of return higher than many after-tax investments. For example, let's say you are doing well and are in a 35 percent federal tax bracket and a 5 percent state tax bracket for a total income tax rate of 40 percent. You shop long and hard for a good money market rate at your local bank and find one willing to pay you 6 percent on your money. However, 40 percent of that income will be lost due to income taxes. Therefore, your 6 percent investment has an effective rate of 3.6 percent. That's not exactly what you signed up for. You'll do much better if you can find a tax-free investment that will return 5 percent. I'll discuss some of these in a later chapter. Adding a few thousand or more tax-free dollars to your portfolio can generate wealth at an amazing clip.

My purpose in giving this quick overview of different types of income is to get you to begin to understand that your situation *can* change if you allow it to. When you work for someone, they issue you a W-2. That is a classic example of earned income. You have no control over the *type* of tax you pay or the *amount* of tax you pay—unless you put some of the income into your company's retirement plan. But when you are self-employed, you have the ability to dictate what type of income you receive. Remember, Barney and Betty made the same dollar amount of income in examples 2, 3, and 4. The reason their taxes were so different in each example was that their *type* of income changed. I constantly push my clients to look for ways to generate types of income that yield preferential tax treatment.

## TYPES OF TAXPAYERS: MAKING CHANGE(S) MEANS MAKING MONEY

Hopefully, by now you are starting to realize that in order to improve your personal tax situation you must make some changes. Let's carry that realization to another level. In the previous section, we briefly discussed different types of income and how those different types could benefit you. Now I want to discuss different types of *taxpayers*. Different types of taxpayers get different types of treatment. This may not sound fair but taxes are not a matter of fairness. Taxes are not a matter of justice. Taxes are not a matter of equality. Taxes are plain and simply a matter of law, period. Let that sink in for a moment. Taxes are a matter of law. A working knowledge of the subject can help you map out a plan to cut your tax bill significantly. Let's begin to acquire some of that knowledge by looking at the different types of taxpayers.

### Individuals

We, as individual taxpayers, are used to one type of taxpayer, aptly called the *individual*. This is your type automatically if you do nothing to change it, and you will be taxed at your full income tax rate *plus* the full 15.3 percent self-employment tax if you have that kind of income. If you are content with your current tax situation, stop reading here. However, if you are ready to see the power of a sophisticated tax plan, keep reading.

### General Partner

A general partner is nothing more than an individual taxpayer who has agreed to go into business with one or more partners. As such, a general partner has the same tax status as an individual taxpayer. You will pay full income tax at whatever bracket you are in *plus* the full 15.3 percent self-employment tax. Merely going into business with others does not create the ability to save taxes on income generated from the business.

To illustrate the tax situation described in these first two examples, let's assume you took your W-2 to your accountant to prepare your taxes. The W-2 reports that you made $30,000. You work hard, you pay the bills, but no one would consider you rich. When your accountant finishes taking deductions for you and your family, the odds are you owe no income taxes. You will receive back all of the income tax you paid in.

Now, let's assume you had your own business and were a general partner. You bring your accountant all of your income and expense receipts and he begins to prepare your tax return. When he is done, your net income from the business is $30,000. When your accountant finishes taking deductions for you and your family, the odds are you will owe no income taxes. However, deductions for you, your family, mortgage interest, charitable contributions, and so on are not permitted for self-employment tax purposes. Therefore, you still must pay 15.3 percent on the entire $30,000 of net income. Quick math says that equates to roughly $4,500 in self-employment tax. Is $4,500 a material amount to someone who makes $30,000 a year? Hopefully, this spells out the problem. Let's start to find some solutions.

## Limited Partner

A limited partner is a partner who invests in a business but has no active participation in the business. A limited partner's share of income is based on her investment, not her personal services. Therefore, a limited partner is not subject to self-employment tax. We could spend hours discussing different methods of utilizing limited partnerships and we will be getting into them in much greater detail in later chapters. Be forewarned however, they are complex. For our purposes here, all I want you to know for the time being is that the use of limited partnerships can significantly reduce self-employment taxes.

## S Corporation Shareholders

An S corporation shareholder is another type of taxpayer defined in the Internal Revenue Code. S corporations are extremely popular for small businesses in which the owner actually works in the business. Unlike individual sole-proprietorships and general partnerships, there is an ability to save significant amounts of self-employment tax by utilizing these entities. An S corporation shareholder is only liable for self-employment taxes on the amount he pays to himself in the form of a salary. This creates an opportunity to provide significant savings when compared with the "default" status of individuals and general partnerships.

## C Corporations

C corporations provide an opportunity to save taxes by utilizing a concept called *income splitting*. The reason for this is that a C corporation pays its own tax. It is its own taxpayer. That means it has its own tax bracket just as individuals do. Like individuals, the C corporation's tax bracket increases as income grows. However, the first $50,000 of C corporation income is taxed at 15 percent. So, if you are in a 35 percent personal tax bracket, the possibility exists of saving significant tax dollars by redirecting some of that income into a C corporation. While this process must be carefully overseen by a tax professional to avoid some inherent pitfalls, the ability to save taxes using C corporations cannot be denied as you will see in later chapters.

## LLC Members

This section would not be complete without a brief mention of an LLC member. An LLC is somewhat of a combination of a partnership and corporation. However, as opposed to the types of taxpayers mentioned earlier, LLC members are not created by federal law. They are created by state law. That poses significant problems in determining exactly how they are taxed. Tax professionals, as well as the IRS, have struggled with this issue for years. The IRS does not make the law. They enforce the law. The challenge is that this is a situation where there is no law to enforce. Don't get too excited. You still have to pay tax on LLC income. Currently, the IRS views LLC members in the same context as general partners. Therefore, LLCs often put taxpayers in a situation where little tax savings occurs. This may be contradictory to what your tax professional has told you, but this is the current way the IRS is leaning. LLCs are great for passive income (i.e., renting property) but not so good for a business in which you actually perform services. We'll be discussing LLCs in much greater detail in later chapters so you will see how you can benefit from their use.

The point of this chapter is to help you realize that depending on how you structure your tax situation, there can be numerous ways to significantly reduce your overall tax bill. Every situation is viewed differently by the IRS based on the application of the categories discussed in this chapter. You must follow a preplanned strategy to make things happen. And that is what each of you must start doing *today*. It's time to move from the status of complaining about your taxes to reducing your taxes. There are indeed steps that you can take, but you must take them.

In the next few chapters, we will be detailing exactly how to go about maximizing the numerous tax deductions available for those who take the time to identify and take advantage of them. The most important advice I have for you is, first work on your individual tax situation and then move to the greatest tax shelter available: owning and operating your own small business. Finally, you can keep things in the family by implementing tax benefits available through family tax planning. The information contained in the next few chapters will make an enormous impact on your road to wealth. Taking the time to learn and implement these strategies will be one of the most important financial decisions you ever make.

# 3

---

# OUTRAGEOUSLY POWERFUL TAX DEDUCTIONS YOU CAN TAKE — WITHOUT OWNING YOUR OWN BUSINESS

Most of you reading this book now are excited to learn about new deductions that can save you money on your taxes. In fact, that may have been one of the main reasons you picked it up in the first place. This chapter deals with personal deductions, or deductions you can take without having your own business. The good news is that there are many deductions and credits that you may not have realized were available to you. The bad news is that not all of these deductions and credits apply to everyone. I like to view personal deductions as *default* deductions. These are the deductions the IRS gives *you* directly. In most cases, they are pre-printed on the tax forms. Common sense states that these default deductions the IRS allows us to take are limited as to just who benefits and how much of a benefit there really is. True tax deductions and more advanced savvy tax planning come from owning your own business. We discuss that in the next chapter, but for now let's focus on personal deductions.

Many people believe that there are no such things as personal deductions. However, the wealthy know that this is not the case and do whatever is necessary to take advantage of any and all deductions. In this chapter, I break these available deductions into three categories:

1. Above-the-line deductions.
2. Itemized deductions.
3. Tax credits.

Many taxpayers fail to realize the differences in these types of tax benefits. To better understand these differences, let's analyze them a little more closely.

## ABOVE-THE-LINE DEDUCTIONS

Above-the-line deductions are commonly referred to as *adjustments to income*. The line refers to your adjusted gross income (AGI). Deductions that occur above the line are available to all taxpayers. Deductions that occur below the line are only available to those taxpayers who itemize their deductions. Above-the-line deductions change annually. In fact, it is not uncommon for an above-the-line deduction to either be added or renewed *after* the tax forms have already been printed and sent to taxpayers. It is important to know what deductions are available to you and, more importantly, how these deductions can save you money.

Remember, your tax preparer is generally aware only of what you give him or her. It is up to you to point out these deductions. The more knowledge you have regarding potential tax-saving strategies the better. Let's look at some of the above-the-line deductions available to you:

### Education, Military, Government

- Grades K-12 teachers, instructors, counselors, principals, and aides can currently deduct up to $250 of out-of-pocket expenses above the line (without itemizing).
- National Guard members and Armed Forces reservists who must travel more than 100 miles away from home and stay overnight

to fulfill their training and service commitments can claim an above-the-line deduction for the cost of transportation, meals, and lodging.
- Government officials employed by a state or local government who are paid in whole or in part on a fee basis can claim business expenses above the line.
- Tuition and fees deductions are missed quite often. Taxpayers realize there are credits available for tuition. And as often is the case, many taxpayers make too much money to be able to take those credits. The tuition and fees deduction allows taxpayers to deduct up to $4,000 of qualified higher education expenses as an above-the-line deduction. So, just because you have phased out of a credit does not mean you have lost the ability to deduct education expenses.
- Up to $2,500 of qualified student loan interest paid can be deducted above the line. As your income increases, this deduction is phased out. However, it can provide some significant tax savings, especially when you are first out of school.

## Health

- Health savings accounts (HSA) are savings accounts set up exclusively for the payment of qualified medical expenses of the account beneficiary or the beneficiary's spouse or dependents. Current contributions to an HSA can be up to $2,700 for an individual plan or $5,450 for a family plan. These contributions can be made up until April 15 of the year following the tax year. So, contributions for 2006 must have been made by April 15, 2007. These contributions to an HSA are above-the-line deductions. If the account is then used to pay for qualified medical expenses, the withdrawals from these accounts are not subject to tax. These accounts turn what would be nondeductible medical expenses into current tax deductions.

- Self-employed individuals can deduct 100 percent of their health insurance premiums above the line.

## Moving Expenses

- The cost of moving household goods and travel expenses for one trip by the taxpayer and each member of the household are deductible above the line. In some cases, temporary storage of household goods can also be deducted. To qualify, the taxpayer's new job location and former house must be at least 50 miles from the old job location and former house. The taxpayer also needs to work as a full-time employee at the new location for at least 39 weeks in the 12-month period following the move. There are some exceptions that will make this deduction available to even more taxpayers. Learn as much as you can about this deduction because it can help reduce the financial strain that often comes with a household move.

## Retirement, Savings, Loans, Alimony

- SEP, SIMPLE, and other qualified plans are specific deductible contributions made for the benefit of a self-employed taxpayer or partner in a partnership. While you would not need a business entity to qualify for these plans, you would need to have your own business and report income from self-employment. These deductions could be as large as $44,000 for both you and your spouse and, in some cases, contributions could be made as late as October 15 of the following year. Now that's leveraging your money.
- An individual with earned income may qualify to contribute up to $4,000 to an individual retirement account (IRA). This amount can be as much as $5,000 for individuals over 50 years old. It is also possible for a spouse who does not have income to make a contribution to an IRA based on the income of the other spouse. You do not have to be self-employed to take advantage of this deduction. Having the ability to contribute to a qualified

retirement plan at work may, however, limit how much you could contribute to an IRA. Contributions to an IRA can be made until April 15 of the following year.

- If you cash in a CD early, the bank will charge you an early withdrawal penalty. This penalty is deductible above the line.

- To be deductible, alimony or separate maintenance payments must be required by a divorce or decree of separation. It is important to note that child support, property settlements, and voluntary payments are *not* deductible alimony.

## Miscellaneous

- For 2006, the domestic producer deduction (DPD) is the lesser of 3 percent of the business's qualified production activities income or 3 percent of the business's taxable income determined without regard to the DPD. That is very confusing, but the deduction can be very real. If you are engaged in a producing activity, such as farming, you may have a deduction available to you that even your tax preparer is not aware of.

- Qualified performing artists can deduct business expenses above the line. There are certain limitations here, but it is worth investigating if you think this deduction may apply to you.

Once again, these are just some of the items available to taxpayers as above-the-line deductions. They are available to basically everyone who qualifies. You do not have to have a corporation and you do not have to itemize your deductions to receive the tax benefits that accompany these deductions.

### ITEMIZED DEDUCTIONS

Perhaps the most common type of money-saving tax strategies for individuals are itemized deductions. Unfortunately, itemized deductions are fast becoming extinct for many middle- and low-income taxpayers. When you file your tax return, you can either take the standard deduction available to you or you can choose to itemize your deductions with a preset list of items the IRS allows you to deduct. Obviously, in making this determination, we want to take the method that gives us the greatest deduction. The standard deduction for a married couple in 2006 was $10,300. That is a significant amount and will continue to be indexed for inflation. However, as the standard deduction goes up, more and more taxpayers are losing the ability to itemize their deductions. In many ways, itemized deductions as we know them are being devalued in our current system. Itemized deductions are available only to those taxpayers (who for now we will assume are married, filing a joint return) who have over $10,300 in itemized expenses. This eliminates a large portion of the population from taking itemized deductions. Remember in the last section we talked about how above-the-line deductions were available to everyone that qualified. That is not the case with itemized deductions. Let's take a look at some of the most common itemized deductions:

- *Medical expenses:* Deducting your medical expenses as an itemized deduction is basically a tax deduction myth. To be deductible, a taxpayer has to first itemize their deductions *and* their medical expenses must *exceed* 7.5 percent of their income. That 7.5 percent threshold takes a huge chunk out of the medical expenses you have. In most cases, this means your medical expenses are not deductible as an itemized deduction. Proper tax planning could allow you to deduct these otherwise nondeductible expenses by utilizing a health savings account (discussed earlier) or a medical reimbursement plan as a fringe benefit through a corporation (discussed in the next chapter).
- *Charitable contributions:* You can deduct up to 50 percent of your total income on contributions you make to qualified charities. These contributions can be either cash or noncash. However, the IRS is beginning to crack down on these deductions. Cash contributions need to be substantiated. A cancelled check does

not constitute substantiation for a contribution that is greater than $250 to any one organization in one day. Those contributions need to be substantiated in writing from the organization that receives the donation.

Household goods and clothing are an easy, effective way to generate some tax deductions that do not require the use of your cash. I would suggest accumulating these items a couple of times a year and taking them to a local charity. Everyone benefits, except the IRS.

- *Taxes:* As bad as taxes can be, one good thing that comes out of them is that they can sometimes be deductible. The following taxes are deductible as itemized deductions:
  - The greater of state/local income taxes or sales taxes paid
  - Real estate taxes
  - Personal property taxes

  In states that do not have a state income tax, taxpayers can deduct the amount of sales taxes they pay to state and local authorities. Just in case you haven't saved all of those receipts, the IRS does have tables that can estimate the amount of sales taxes you have paid based on your income, where you live, and the number of people in your family. If you live in a state that has a state income tax, you can deduct the greater of the income tax or the sales tax, but not both, as an itemized deduction.

Mortgage interest is deductible on your principal residence and on a second (vacation) home. Interest on a third home would be nondeductible personal interest. Home equity interest is generally limited to $100,000 of debt for the main and second home combined. Just because you refinance your home or take out a second mortgage does not mean the interest is automatically deductible in full. Please get advice from your tax preparer before making what could be an incorrect assumption.

Points and loan origination fees are generally deductible on the purchase of a principal residence in the year the residence is purchased. This can generate large extra deductions. Generally, the amount deductible will be about 1 percent of the amount financed. If you finance $200,000 on your new residence, you will likely have a $2,000 tax deduction the first year. There are some rules to meet, just know that this could be a hidden deduction you are entitled to take.

Points and loan origination fees paid to refinance are *not* deductible in full the first year. Instead, they must be spread over the term of the loan. If you refinance your home for 15 years, you can take 1/15 of the points and loan origination fees paid per year. However, if you later refinance that loan again with a different lending institution, the amount of these fees that have not yet been deducted now become fully deductible. Many taxpayers miss this deduction every year.

With the recent fluctuations in interest rates, millions of Americans have refinanced homes once, twice, or even three or more times. There are undoubtedly millions of dollars of tax deductions that have not yet been claimed. Remember, you have three years to amend a federal tax return if you discover that you missed out on some potential deductions to which you may have been entitled.

Investment interest is interest paid on borrowed money used to buy investments including stocks, bonds, mutual funds, and even real estate. One type of investment interest that is often missed is margin interest that is paid in investment accounts. Investment interest is deductible up to the amount of net investment income received. Any excess amounts can be carried over to subsequent years.

Gifts of appreciated property are a way to generate a double deduction, so to speak. Let's say that you wanted to donate $10,000 to your local church. After analyzing your portfolio, you determine that in order to accomplish your financial objectives, you need to sell $15,000 worth of stock you purchased a few years back for $9,000. Doing so would result in a $6,000 capital gain that you would have to pay tax on and a deductible contribution of $10,000. What would happen if you simply gave the church $10,000 worth of stock? The answer is a *double* tax savings bonus. You still get the same $10,000 tax deduction, but you do not have to report any capital gains. Wealthy people always seek to take advantages of these opportunities. Shouldn't you?

Casualty losses are losses that occur from an identifiable event that is sudden, unexpected, or unusual, such as fires, earthquakes, floods, tornadoes, hurricanes, storms, theft, vandalism, and even car accidents. While there are some limits as to what is deductible, losses that come from these types of events can be substantial. The ability to deduct these types of losses can generate a great deal of tax savings.

Some miscellaneous deductions are deductible in full. Others are subject to a 2 percent of income phase-out. This works just like the 7.5 percent phase-out of medical expenses we talked about earlier. Once these expenses are greater than 2 percent of your income, the excess is allowed as an itemized deduction. Fully deductible miscellaneous itemized deductions include:

- Gambling losses to the extent of gambling winnings
- Certain job-related expenses of the handicapped
- Estate tax imposed on taxable income (income in respect of a decedent)
- Unrecovered cost of annuities on a decedent's last return
- Repayments of income (such as social security benefits or unemployment)

Miscellaneous itemized deductions that are subject to a 2 percent phase-out include:

- Appraisal fees (for charitable donations and casualty losses)
- Employee business expense
- Fees to collect interest or dividends
- Hobby expenses, up to the amount of hobby income
- Investment expenses
- Job Search expenses
- Certain legal fees
- Job related education expenses
- Professional and union dues

- Safe deposit box fees
- Cost of installing a safe in a home
- Tax preparation or other tax assistance expenses
- Work clothes and uniforms required for your job and not suitable for street wear

While this is not an exhaustive list, you can see that there are many types of expenses that fall under this category.

There are a number of miscellaneous itemized deductions that can be taken in connection with your employment. Unreimbursed employee expenses, such as mileage, travel, meals, cell phone charges, and perhaps even uniforms and work clothes can be deducted as an itemized deduction. Job search expenses also qualify in this category, as does job-related education if the education does not help you meet the minimum requirement for your job or qualify you for a new job.

Basically, if you have out-of-pocket costs associated with your employment, there is a very good chance that these expenses are somehow tax deductible. You owe it to yourself to find out.

## Tax Credits

*Tax credits* are the best type of tax savings. A credit is a dollar-for-dollar savings. If you are entitled to a $1,000 credit, you save $1,000 on your tax bill. If you receive a $1,000 tax deduction your tax savings is based upon your incremental tax rate. If you are in a 25 percent tax bracket, your tax savings would be $250 on a $1,000 tax deduction. So as you can see, tax credits can be huge.

Some tax credits are the same year after year. However, some credits come and go regularly. Congress likes to create tax incentives every so often to encourage taxpayers to save for retirement, purchase fuel-efficient automobiles, or even install energy-efficient windows. Often, these credits are for a limited time. It is imperative that you stay up to date with what credits the tax code currently has to offer on an annual basis in order to maximize your benefits.

Some tax credits are personal in nature (such as child tax or child care credits) while some credits are of a business nature. For example, did you know that there is a credit available for small employers who establish a new retirement plan for their business? This credit could equal 50 percent of the cost of establishing the plan. Once again, this is not a credit that everyone would know about. You have to always put yourself in a position to take advantage of these opportunities.

Credits are also used extensively in disaster areas to help revitalize the economy. There are numerous additional credits available for certain real estate investments and even educational expenses in the Hurricane Katrina disaster areas. These areas are commonly referred to as a "go zone." The same was true in New York after 9/11.

Table 3.1 summarizes some of the personal tax credits that are available to taxpayers. While there may be additional business credits, these personal credits do cover a wide range of activities. My guess is that if you look closely, you can find a credit that may be available to you.

## Other Personal Tax Planning Strategies

When it comes to personal tax planning, there may be no better tax shelter than owning your own home. In fact, many wealthy families use their personal residence as a wealth-building vehicle. Selling your personal residence at a gain may very well be the single, largest source of *tax-free income* for those taxpayers who qualify. That's correct. These gains can be *tax-free*.

A single taxpayer can exclude up to $250,000 of gain from the sale of a personal residence if the individual owned and used the home as a principal residence for at least two out of the five years prior to the sale. Married taxpayers may be able to exclude up to $500,000 of gain from the sale of their personal residence. This exclusion applies to only one sale every two years.

One thing you will find is that tax considerations are always on the mind of the wealthy. Adopting this mindset can make you money.

**Table 3.1 Personal Tax Credits Available to Taxpayers**

| Tax Credit | For | Amount |
|---|---|---|
| Additional Child Tax Credit | Taxpayers who don't claim full $1,000 tax credit for each child and have (1) one or more qualifying children and over $11,300 of earned income or (2) three or more qualifying children. | Up to $1,000 per child. |
| Adoption Expense Credit | Expenses incurred in the legal adoption of a child under age 18 or the adoption of an incapacitated or special needs person (regardless of age). | Up to $10,960 per eligible child. |
| Alternative Motor Vehicle Credit | Four categories of new vehicles, the most common being hybrid vehicles, placed in service after 2005. | Up to $3,400 for hybrids; various limits for other types. |
| Child and Dependent Care Credit | Day care expenses for dependent(s) (under age 13 or incapacitated) that allow taxpayer to work or look for work. | 20% to 35% of qualifying expenses depending on AGI level. |
| Child Tax Credit | Taxpayers with qualifying children under age 17. | Up to $1,000 per child. |
| Credit for the Elderly or the Disabled | Low-income taxpayers age 65 or older or permanently and totally disabled. Nontaxable Social Security (or equivalent) must be less than $7,500 MFJ if both spouses eligible. | Based on filing status, age and income. For MFJ also based on spouse's age and income. |
| Earned Income Credit | Working families with this many children:<br>One—AGI less than $32,001 ($34,001 if MFJ).<br>Two +—AGI less than $36,348 ($38,348 if MFJ).<br>None:—AGI less than $12,120 ($14, 120 if MFJ). | Maximum Credit:<br>$2,747 for one child.<br>$4,536 for two children.<br>$412 for no children. |
| Education Credits (Hope Scholarship Credit; Lifetime Learning Credit) | Qualified college or vocational school expenses for eligible students. | Hope: Up to $1,650 per student. Lifetime Learning: 20% of first $10,000 of expenses per return. |

| Credit | Description | Amount |
|---|---|---|
| Electric Vehicle | New qualified electric vehicle placed in service during 2006. | 10% of cost $1,000 maximum. |
| Federal Tax Paid on Fuels | Fuels used on a farm for farming purposes, off-highway business use and other qualified uses. | Varies by type of fuel and use. |
| Foreign Tax Credit | Income taxes paid to a foreign country or U.S. possession on income that is also subject to U.S. federal income tax. | Amount of foreign tax not exceeding U.S. tax multiplied by ratio of foreign/total taxable income. |
| Health Coverage Tax Credit | Individuals eligible to receive trade adjustment allowance or who receive pension benefits from the PBGC. | 65% of qualified health insurance costs. |
| Minimum Tax Credit | Credit allowed against regular tax for part of the alternative minimum tax (AMT) paid and attributable to deferral items (timing preferences and adjustments). | AMT attributable to deferral items. |
| Mortgage Interest Credit | Part of interest expense paid by homebuyers issued a government mortgage credit certificate. | Based on interest paid and credit rate under certificate. |
| Nonbusiness Energy Property Credit | 1) Qualified energy efficiency improvements. 2) Residential energy property expenditures. | 1) 10% of expenditures. 2) 100% of expenditures. Combined lifetime limit of $500. |
| Residential Energy Efficient Property Credit | Qualified photovoltaic property. Qualified solar water heating property. Qualified fuel cell property. | 1) 30%; $2,000 credit limit. 2) 30%; $2,000 credit limit. 3) 30%; $1,000 per kilowatt limit. |
| Retirement Savings Contributions Credit | Credit for low-income and middle-income individuals who make retirement plan contributions. Credit in addition to tax deduction. | 10% to 50% of contributions (≤$2,000). AGI ≤$50,000 MFJ, $37,500 HOH, $25,000 other. |

Decisions as to when to go house hunting become even more important. Doing so a few months too early could cost you big bucks in tax savings. Make sure you understand the rules and make sure you have consulted your tax advisor when planning on utilizing this powerful tax-saving strategy.

There is also tax planning involved in transferring assets from generation to generation. While I do not intend on going through a detailed estate planning scenario here, I do want to point out the difference between receiving assets through inheritance versus simply transferring or gifting assets before death. Many taxpayers do not handle these situations properly which ends up costing them thousands of dollars in taxes, even with a small estate.

Let's take a look at how this information can help us. Assets that are gifted are received at the donor's (person doing the gifting) basis. Inherited property is received with a basis equal to the fair market value (FMV) of the asset at the date of death. For example, let's say your parents want to get a rental property they own out of their name and into yours in order to make the transition after death easier. So, they go through the motions and actually transfer title to the property into your name. Let's say that the property was purchased 25 years ago at a cost to your parents of $20,000. Today it is worth $150,000. In this scenario, your basis in the property is the basis your parents had, $20,000. After their death, you decide that you really don't want the hassle of keeping up with the rental property so you sell it at fair market value, or $150,000. Set up in this manner, you now have a taxable gain of $130,000 ($150,000 FMV less $20,000 basis).

Now, however, let's assume that your parents did not transfer title of the property to you during their lifetime. Instead, you inherited the property at your parents' death. Under this scenario, your basis now becomes the fair market value of the property at the date of death. Your basis is now $150,000. You sell the property at FMV, $150,000. You have no gain and therefore pay no tax on this transaction. In fact, you very likely have a loss due to the closing costs incurred upon the sale.

This example can work with real estate, stocks, investments, and even collectibles. Please consult competent tax advisors when planning your estate or the estate of your parents. I guarantee you they will more than pay for themselves.

While we have certainly not covered every imaginable scenario available for reducing taxes, you should understand that there are indeed ways to pay less of your money out in taxes. In the next chapter, we'll take a peek behind the curtain at the greatest tax shelter in the world today: owning and operating your own small business.

# 4

---

# THE GREATEST TAX SHELTER IN THE WORLD

## *Owning Your Own Business*

While understanding how to maximize your personal deductions and credits can save you a substantial amount of money, this chapter kicks things into high gear. The information in this chapter is geared toward individuals who really want to take it to the next level of savings. The best advice I can give to anyone looking to keep a larger percentage of their hard-earned money is to do what it takes to *own your own business*. Owning your own business does not have to mean owning your own Fortune 500 Company or having to deal with a bunch of employees. Owning your own business is simply finding an activity or service you enjoy doing, developing a profit motive, and putting that plan into practice. This is one of the secrets that enable the wealthy to drastically reduce, and even eliminate, a good portion of their tax bill.

When you own your own business, *you* determine how much income you pay taxes on. Simply put, if you want to pay less in taxes, you have to come up with more deductions. As we discussed in the previous chapter, personal deductions are severely limited and not all deductions apply to all taxpayers. Business deductions, on the other hand, are limited to all "ordinary and necessary" business expenses. As you can imagine, this can be a very exhaustive list. The larger that list, the larger the amount of money left in your pocket.

## Having Your Cake and Eating It Too with Tax-Free Fringe Benefits

Let's start with some basic, but extremely powerful, business deductions. A common form of business for successful companies is a C corporation. A C corporation has many differences from other forms of business that we discussed in Chapter 3. One major difference is the ability of the C corporation to deduct certain fringe benefits. You may be wondering, "What constitutes a fringe benefit?" The IRS defines a fringe benefit as certain types of compensation or other benefit received by an employee that is not payable in the form of cash. These types of expenses can become tax-saving tools for owners of C corporations. Although these expenses may be costs that occur regularly in your business, in other forms of business they may simply be nondeductible personal expenses. Through a C corporation these nondeductible expenses can be converted into instant tax deductions. Let's look at some examples of fringe benefits:

- Health insurance
- Medical reimbursement plans
- Cafeteria plans
- Educational assistance
- Child care assistance
- Adoption assistance
- Employer-provided vehicles
- Group term life insurance
- Qualified moving expense reimbursement
- Qualified retirement plans

- Retirement planning services
- Deferred compensation

While this is certainly not an exhaustive list, my guess is that you are spending considerable amounts of money on at least one of these items currently on an after-tax basis. If so, don't continue to let this tax-saving strategy get past you. This one tactic could help you save hundreds, if not thousands, in taxes each and every year.

## RETIREMENT PLAN POWER

If I told you that there is a tax deduction available to your business that could help you retire as a millionaire, would you be interested? Of course you would. Well, let me tell you that one of the largest deductions available to a business is a retirement plan. It continually amazes me how many taxpayers fail to take advantage of this tremendous tax-saving, wealth-building tool.

In today's society, we have many claims on our money. We have mortgages, utilities, transportation, insurance, education, taxes, and the list goes on and on. Maximizing your retirement plan adds yet another item to the list. When you sit down and prepare your household budget, my guess is that retirement planning, for most individuals, is the left over amount after paying for everything else. If there is nothing left over, you decide to deal with retirement planning later. As we all know, later may not come until it is already too late. I learned something very valuable from one of my mentors years ago. He said to me, "If you will do for a few years what most people won't do, you can do for the rest of your life what most people can't do." This lesson has made an enormous impact on my financial life as well as on the lives of many of my clients. It is especially appropriate when discussing retirement plans.

Let's first look at retirement planning from a practical tax-saving strategy. I will make the assumption that we are in a 30 percent combined federal *and* state tax bracket. If we put $1,000 into a retirement plan, we have saved $300 in taxes in the current year. The government is essentially giving us money to help us save for our future. Why do so many people fail to realize this? In 2007, the maximum amount of income we can defer into a retirement plan is $44,000 per person. That's right, you and your spouse can each contribute up to $44,000 per year to a retirement plan. Do the math, how much tax are you saving?

A second, but equally powerful, part of retirement planning is the tax-free growth. A consistent, patient approach to retirement planning can amass a tremendous amount of wealth. If you have ever done any research on financial planning or investing, you have most likely come across the Rule of 72. For those of you who haven't, it works like this: Take your expected rate of return on an investment and divide that number into 72. The result is how long it takes your money to double. For example, if you think your return on an investment will be 10 percent, take 72 and divide it by 10, the result is 7.2. In other words, it would take 7.2 years for your money to double assuming a 10 percent return.

Now, let's say you are 35 years old, you contribute $5,000 to a retirement plan this year, and you expect to earn 10 percent on your money over time. Using the Rule of 72, how would this investment look when you retire?

| | |
|---|---|
| Age 42 | $10,000 |
| Age 49 | $20,000 |
| Age 56 | $40,000 |
| Age 63 | $80,000 |

As you can see, about the time that retirement thoughts start to enter your mind, your initial investment has grown to approximately $80,000. The amazing thing with the above scenario is that it is assuming a *one-time* contribution of $5,000. What if you contributed $5,000 every year? What if your spouse put in $5,000 as well? What if you put in even more? The point I want to focus on is whether you can contribute $5,000 or $500, a retirement plan can not only save a significant amount of taxes, it can also put you well on your way to financial freedom.

## Minor Deductions Mean Major Savings

Some of the best tax deductions you may have never utilized are perhaps right under your nose, and I mean literally, right under your nose. Do you realize how much of a tax deduction your children can be to your business? I'm not talking about personal exemptions or child tax credits that are available to all taxpayers. I'm talking about incorporating your children into your business.

How much can your children earn without having to pay income tax? Currently, the amount is a little over $5,000, but for simplicity sake we will use the $5,000 amount. Yes, your child can earn $5,000 and pay no income tax. This income can come from a part-time, after-school job, a summer job, or working for you in your business. That's right, you can take a deduction for paying your kids to perform services for your business.

Perhaps you have a child in college. If this is the case, my guess is that occasionally you may have to send him or her money for expenses that arise. In this way, this payment is a nondeductible personal expense. What if you had your child perform some service for your business? As long as this payment was "ordinary and necessary" to your business, the payment to your child would be tax deductible to your business and nontaxable to your child as long as he or she earned less than $5,000. How big a deal is this? Let's take a look.

If you are in a 30 percent tax bracket, paying your child $5,000 for services he or she performed in your business would save you $1,500 in taxes. That's real money. Now, how many children do you have? Simple math says it does not take long for these potential deductions to add up to significant tax savings.

You may not know it, but your children are also eligible to contribute up to $4,000 to an IRA if they have earned income. This could be a traditional (deductible) IRA or a Roth IRA. So, you could pay your child $9,000. Your child could contribute $4,000 to his or her traditional IRA. Your child would then have $5,000 of taxable income. As we just discussed, if this is all the income your child has, they will owe no tax. How would a $9,000 deduction help your tax situation? Even better, how would it help your child in the long run. The multiple advantages associated with these strategies are what enable the wealthy to get and stay that way.

In the previous example, your $9,000 payment to your child would save you $2,700, assuming a 30 percent tax bracket. Your child could start a traditional IRA and contribute $4,000. Your child could then use the remaining $5,000 to begin saving for college. You could save taxes, plan for your child's education, and plan for the financial future. That is a pretty good year, wouldn't you say?

Whether you could maximize this potential tax strategy or only implement a fraction of it, you can still generate substantial deductions by incorporating your kids into your business. By planning properly, the right entity structure can even make these payments to your children free of Social Security and Medicare taxes. Planning like this is what makes your tax planning team worth every penny. The money that you spend on tax and other financial advice and assistance is an investment. The wealthy understand this and don't find themselves doing what I refer to as, "tripping over pennies on their way to dollars."

## Income Shifting for Tax Savings

Our tax system is based on incremental tax rates. You may have heard this term before but chances are you don't really know what it means. Basically, once your income goes over a certain threshold, any amount of money you make over that threshold is taxed at a higher rate. Some taxpayers in a 25 percent tax bracket may believe all of the taxable income is taxed at 25 percent. That is incorrect. They would have some income taxed at 0 percent, some at 10 percent, some at 15 percent, and some at 25 percent. Income shifting is the process of taking income out of your bracket (in this example, 25 percent) and shifting it to someone else. Tax savings can occur when this shifting is done to someone or *some entity* that is in a lower tax bracket.

Income shifting is very common within families. Within a given family unit, you most likely have varying tax brackets among the different individuals. *Business tax planning* gives you the ability to shift income from individuals in high tax brackets to individuals in lower tax brackets. If the process seems simple to you, that's because it is. Basic elementary math proves this strategy can save you (and your family) an abundance of tax dollars.

## Real Estate Riches

As you might imagine, I am an avid follower of the business strategies of Donald Trump. I especially appreciate the information he teaches in the field of real estate. There are very few business opportunities that allow you to build wealth without paying taxes and then subsequently pay reduced rates when the time comes to settle up with Uncle Sam. Real estate, however, is a prime exception.

While real estate entrepreneurs will teach that there are multiple ways to make money with real estate, for our purposes, we will focus on the two most common; rental income and appreciation. Set up properly, both of these wealth-building tools will result in little to no tax due until the property is sold.

Let's assume you purchased a rental property for $100,000 and you found a tenant who paid $1,100 rent per month. Your monthly out-of-pocket expenses averaged $1,000. This would include mortgage payments, repairs, management fees, and so on. While this scenario does generate some positive cash flow (cash inflows greater than cash outflows), this will most likely result in a tax loss. The reason for this is that when you file this activity on your tax return, you are entitled to *depreciate* your property. Depreciation allows you to recoup the purchase price of your property over time through annual tax deductions. In other words, depreciation is a noncash expense. Combining depreciation with other rental expenses may very well mean that your total expenses exceed the amount of cash you have actually spent out of pocket on the rental activity. In some situations, this tax loss can be used to offset other W-2 income. The bottom line to you is that you receive valuable tax benefits. The wealthy realize this which explains part of the reason that they are so actively involved in real estate.

The second wealth-building aspect in this example would be the appreciation of the property itself. Over time, real estate values tend to increase. Let's assume that over a three-year period the property we purchased has increased in value to $120,000. The monthly mortgage payments made on the property have reduced the outstanding debt to $95,000. You now have increased your net worth by $25,000 without paying a dime in tax. Are you starting to see why the wealthy are involved in real estate? They're not in real estate because they are wealthy, they're wealthy because they're in real estate.

Another exciting part of this scenario is that when the property is eventually sold to turn that equity into cash, the majority of the gain will be taxed as a long-term capital gain that has preferential tax treatment. Currently, the maximum long-term capital gain rate is 15 percent. Remember how we talked about business owners being able to dictate the type of income they receive? If you went out and got a second job that paid $25,000, odds are after paying all of the taxes due on that additional income (federal and state income tax, Social Security, and Medicare) you would be paying close to 40 percent in taxes. Using this wealth-building real estate tool, you would only be paying around 20 percent assuming you live in a state with state income tax. That's half the tax on the same dollar amount of income. That's solid tax planning, which means a solid increase in the amount of money in your pocket.

## Paying Zero Percent Capital Gains

While the real estate example may excite you, some of you may still not like having to pay tax at all, even at preferential rates. Would you be interested in avoiding paying the tax on the sale of your property completely while maintaining or even increasing your overall net worth? Of course, any wise investor would. Amazingly, this can indeed happen and even better, it is *totally legal*.

Any investor in real estate needs to know about §1031, or like-kind, exchanges. A like-kind exchange allows you to sell a property at a gain and then roll that gain into a like-kind property. The gain generated by the first transaction is deferred into the new property. In other words, you will owe *no* tax on the sale of your property using §1031. If you later sell the acquired property at a gain, tax would be due at that time. What if you did another §1031 exchange at that time? Once again, you would defer the tax. Any portion of the tax code that legally allows you to not pay tax *must* be taken advantage of.

It's important to note that "like-kind" property does not mean that the property must be the same as the previous property. Basically, any business or investment property would qualify. You could sell the rental property we talked about earlier and acquire vacant land, a strip shopping center, or a duplex. You are not limited to exchanging a single-family residence for a single-family residence. You can also turn three small properties into one, larger property. This flexibility allows you to take your investments in basically any direction you want *and* pay no to current taxes.

There are some rules that apply to a §1031 exchange. This exchange must be done at the time of sale. A §1031 exchange does not occur in your accountants' office at tax time. Everyone involved (buyer, seller, accountant, real estate agent, and title company) needs to know *before* the transaction occurs that you intend this transaction to be part of a §1031 exchange. There are a few important timelines with §1031 exchanges. The key right now is not to memorize all of the ins and outs of a §1031 exchange. The key is to know they exist and have a tax-planning team who can help you take advantage of this tremendous tax break.

## SECRET OF COST SEGREGATION

Real estate entrepreneurs have many advantages in the tax code. Think of some of the wealthiest people you know. I would guess that these individuals have significant activities in real estate. This is no coincidence. Rich people know how to take advantage of their tax situation. This is part of the reason they're rich. They also know about insider secrets that most people don't know about. One of those secrets is *cost segregation*.

Cost segregation is a very underutilized real estate option. Cost segregation has to do with depreciation. Remember, depreciation allows you to recoup the purchase price of your property over time through annual tax deductions. Depreciation is required for all assets purchased and placed in service in your business. Assets such as business and commercial property are depreciated over 27.5 years and 39 years accordingly. Personal assets such as business equipment, computers, furniture, and so on are generally depreciated over 5 or 7 years.

As you can see, there is a significant difference in these depreciation periods. When you purchase residential property, that property is depreciated over 27.5 years. That is a long time. Perhaps your tax situation requires that you look for every advantage the tax code offers. Let's think about what you just purchased when you acquired that residential rental property. You purchased the physical structure, but you also purchased the refrigerator, stove, microwave, light fixture, and maybe even a washer and dryer. These assets are eligible to be depreciated over 5 or 7 years. Tax savings can be generated by simply allocating the purchase price to these various items. This can front-load your depreciation deductions to generate current tax deductions that you would otherwise have to wait 27 or 39 years to take. This gives you a larger current deduction to maximize your current tax savings.

## LET'S GET FISCAL

A corporate form of business will allow you to choose an off calendar fiscal year end. This is simply a tax year that ends sometime other than December 31. This can create opportunities for you to determine when you pay tax and when you take deductions. What's the benefit?

Let's say you had a C corporation with a fiscal year end of January 31, 2007. As a taxpaying individual, your year-end is December 31, 2006. Can this scenario give you any tax benefit?

If your corporation paid you a bonus during December 2006, when would you have to file and pay taxes on that money? As an individual, that tax would be due April 15, 2007. Let's assume the corporation paid you a bonus in January 2007. When is your tax due now? It would not be due until April 15, *2008*. However, the C corporation would get the benefit of the tax deduction when its tax return is due—*March 15, 2007*. Properly utilizing this strategy can allow you to receive the benefit of a tax deduction a full year before the income is reported and tax is paid to Uncle Sam. Could you put that money to better use than your Uncle? Here's your chance.

## PLANNING AHEAD FOR YEAR-END PLANNING

As a society, we procrastinate all the time. Never is this more evident than in our annual tax planning. To millions of business owners, tax planning starts on New Year's Eve. While I am a strong advocate of year-round tax planning, there are some things that can be done at year-end to reduce the impending tax bill.

In a business, you get to choose whether you will be a *cash basis taxpayer* or an *accrual basis taxpayer*. A cash basis taxpayer records (or pays taxes on) income when it is received and deducts expenses when they are paid. Taxpayers using this method will often load up on expenses at the end of the year. Perhaps you know that your five year old computer will need to be replaced soon. Purchasing that computer in December can help speed up the tax deduction you are entitled to receive.

An accrual basis taxpayer, on the other hand, reports income when it is earned and deducts expenses when they are incurred. What this means is if you earn the money it's taxable even if it has not yet been received. What this also means is if you purchase something, it is deductible, even if you have not yet paid for it. This creates several good cash flow options for deducting expenses. Let's take a look at some of these options.

Let's say that the year is winding down and you are worried that your tax bill will be more than expected. You want to generate some tax deductions, but you are short on cash. It is after all the end of the year and the cash you have is needed elsewhere. When evaluating your business needs you determine that you could improve your efficiency if you purchased new computer equipment and office furniture. You do some shopping and determine that the equipment that will best benefit your business will cost you $10,000. The problem is that you don't have $10,000 in cash. You can purchase the equipment and furniture using a credit card or revolving charge account and take a tax deduction for the full amount without having paid a dime out of pocket. Of course, as the debt is paid back there is no deduction, but who cares? You have just front-loaded a $10,000 deduction without paying any cash in the current year. The IRS has basically given you an interest-free loan. It's strategies like these that the rich know about that others don't. It's strategies like these that help them keep more of their money so that they can make even more money.

## SECTION 179 DEPRECIATION MAGIC

The depreciation deduction under §179 has been referred to as "the mother of all tax deductions." While it has been around for a long time, it is currently giving us the greatest tax benefit it ever has. What is it? §179 allows a business owner to currently deduct up to $108,000 of assets purchased and placed in service in the business during the year. Earlier, I said that assets must be depreciated over time, but this section of the tax code short-circuits that requirement.

Combining the depreciation benefits of §179, with the accrual basis method of accounting mentioned earlier, could potentially allow a business owner to deduct up to $108,000 of asset purchases while actually spending little to no money now. It does not take a mathematician to see the super-charged tax benefits that can be gained from properly utilizing this section. Some examples of assets that fall under §179 include but are not limited to:

- Airplanes
- Automobiles
- Computers
- Computer software
- Fences in a farming business
- Livestock
- Machinery and equipment
- Moveable signs
- Office equipment
- Office furniture
- Oil and gas well and drilling equipment
- Store counters
- Tractors

Be aware that the benefits under §179 will not be around at this level forever and future Congresses can, and most likely will, change the benefits available under §179. Proper planning can ensure that you can maximize the tax benefits available to you by utilizing this incredibly powerful strategy.

These strategies are one of the primary reasons why people make statements such as, "the rich just keep getting richer." It's true. The difference between the rich and others is that the rich take the time to learn the system. Others simply sit around and complain about the system. If you feel like the rules of the game discriminate against one group or another, you're right. Businesses get far more in deductions than do individuals. If you don't like the treatment that you're getting as an individual, it's time for you to get down to business. You can do that by starting a business so that you can take advantage of the tax secrets of the wealthy.

# 5

---

# CREATING A TAX MESS (MULTIPLE ENTITY STRUCTURING STRATEGY)

We have now spent three consecutive chapters talking about different ways to save tremendous amounts of tax dollars using various types of income, business entities, and personal and business tax deductions. This chapter is designed to bring it all together.

It's one thing to know about the tax advantages of passive income, or S corporations, or deducting payments to children, or what types of personal tax credits are available to you. It's another thing entirely to put that knowledge to work for you. The sad reality is that the vast majority of people will do nothing to improve their personal tax situation. To do so takes action. And action is often uncomfortable. If you fall into this category, I hope you have learned something so far or that I have at least piqued your interest in lessening your tax burden. I wish you well in all your business efforts. For those of you who want to implement a tax savings plan, I encourage you to read and reread what has already been presented and take the steps necessary to put your tax multiple entity structuring strategy (MESS) into place.

When I mentioned business entities earlier in this book, I mentioned several types of business entities. You do have a number of options when choosing which business entity works best for your specific situation. To review, those options include:

- General partnership
- Limited partnership
- C corporation
- S corporation
- Limited liability company (LLC)

Although it might be easier to simply talk about just one type of business entity, we have to talk about five different types of entities because there is not one that does everything we need it to do:

1. A general partnership is a great entity in which to own real estate from a tax perspective. However, this is not a recommended entity in which to do business because the individual partners have no liability protection and the general partners will pay maximum self-employment tax on their earned income.
2. A limited partnership provides liability protection to the limited partners, but the limited partners cannot operate, manage, or work in the business and a limited partnership still must have a general partner that has unlimited liability *and* self-employment tax.
3. C corporations are great for big business and for asset protection and income splitting. However, they are not good entities in which to own real estate or assets.
4. S corporations are great for businesses that generate earned income. However, S corporations are generally not good entities in which to own property and there is a requirement that owners who perform services must be put on payroll.
5. LLCs are great entities for owning real estate, but they are not good entities to operate a business that generates earned income.

The bottom line is that each entity has its advantages and each entity has its disadvantages. The key to a successful tax strategy is identifying and utilizing the advantages that work for you while at the same time avoiding the disadvantages.

For example, let's assume you own your own retail business. You sell golf clubs to the public. Let's also assume you own the building in which the business is located. An uneducated entrepreneur would view this as a single business operation. However, there are many tax-saving and wealth-building opportunities here for those who take the time to learn how to access these opportunities.

The first would be the retail sale of golf clubs. The income from this type of business activity would be considered earned income. That means that if this activity was run as a sole proprietorship the entire amount of income would be subject to the 15.3 percent self-employment tax *in addition* to any federal and state income taxes that would be due. Let's analyze the different types of entities to determine which is best for this type of operation.

## General Partnership

A general partnership gives us no liability protection. There would be no distinction between your business assets and your personal assets. If you were to get sued, everything would be at risk. A general partnership must also pay the full 15.3 percent self-employment tax on the business income in addition to federal and state income taxes. In summary, a general partnership gives you no liability protection and maximum taxation. I would not recommend this option.

## Limited Partnership

A limited partnership has two types of partners. The general partner(s) would have the same problems we just talked about: unlimited liability and maximum taxation. The limited partner(s) do have some benefits. The most obvious benefit is that the limited partner is only liable for their investment in the business. Unsecured creditors could not access your personal assets. Limited partners are also not subject to the 15.3 percent self-employment tax. However, limited partners cannot perform any work in the business. They cannot manage the business. They cannot make management decisions. Basically, all they can do is invest money and wait on a return on their investment. This creates a big stumbling block in my example. I would not recommend a limited partnership to sell the golf equipment.

## C CORPORATION

A C corporation definitely gives you the asset protection aspects you are looking for in a business structure. If you remember, the C corporation is the only entity that pays its own tax since it has its own tax bracket. The first $50,000 of income is taxed at 15 percent. Income splitting gives you the ability to save some tax. However, in this example, you most likely would be directing the majority of the income to yourself to pay personal expenses that would not provide the optimal tax treatment. Therefore, a C corporation would not be my first choice of entity to sell the golf clubs.

## LIMITED LIABILITY COMPANY (LLC)

An LLC seems to be the entity of choice today. However, people often form LLCs out of convenience and do not bother looking at the tax aspects. An LLC would provide the assets protection you are looking for in this situation. However, because the income generated from selling golf clubs is considered earned income, you will also be required to pay the 15.3 percent self-employment tax on that income. LLCs are generally not good entities to run businesses that have earned income.

## S Corporation

An S corporation is a corporation that has elected tax treatment under Subchapter S of the Internal Revenue Code. It is still a corporation so it has the same asset protection features of a C corporation. However, an S corporation is a pass-through tax entity. It does not pay its own tax at its own bracket like a C corporation. The big advantage that an S corporation has over other entities is the ability to reduce the 15.3 percent self-employment tax on earned income. In an S corporation, you would need to take a "reasonable" salary for the services you performed. However, income over and above that salary is not subject to the 15.3 percent self-employment tax.

Remember earlier we said that 15.3 percent self-employment tax is due on earned income, or income you receive for your personal services. In our example of selling golf clubs, some of the bottom line income is generated because of your personal services. However, some of the bottom line income is generated from other things such as the personal services of your employees, marketing, your business locations, your pricing strategy, and other expenses. An S corporation allows you to take some of your income subject to the 15.3 percent self-employment tax and some of your income not subject to the 15.3 percent self-employment tax thereby providing you with an opportunity for tax savings. Remember, the rule you have to follow is that you must take a *reasonable* salary for your services.

As you have already figured out, the lower the salary, the lower the self-employment tax. We could spend an entire book attempting to define reasonable salary. Unfortunately, the IRS gives us no parameters. Generally, the IRS looks at what you would earn performing the same job as an employee for someone else. For the purposes of this book, I don't want to be concerned with how much salary to take. I would rather focus on the fact that an S corporation, in the earlier mentioned type of business, appears to be able to save us more overall taxes than our other options.

But let's take a closer look at the overall picture. Let's say that your net income from the sale of golf clubs for a given year is $80,000. Under a sole proprietorship, general partnership, and LLC, you would be subject to the 15.3 percent self-employment tax on this income. Quick math concludes that would cost you a little more than $12,000 in self-employment tax *before* you have paid the first dime in federal or state income tax.

Now let's assume that you operated the business as an S corporation and earned the same $80,000. Let's also assume that you and your accountant determined that a reasonable salary for your services was $50,000. That leaves $30,000 to be taken as a distribution of profits. This distribution of profits is not subject to self-employment taxes. That saves you $4,590 ($30,000 x 15.3 percent). Is $4,590 a material amount to someone who makes $80,000? Given all of our options, I would choose an S corporation as the entity that is in the business of selling golf clubs. However, we don't want to stop there. We've got some more structuring to do.

The second business activity you have going in this example would be the ownership of the building and land. Too many times business owners do not see the opportunity of splitting the activity off from the other operation, in this case selling golf clubs. Just as we did with the retail activity of selling the golf clubs, let's determine what entity would be best to own the property.

Let's first make sure we understand what is taking place. The S corporation that we have formed to run the golf club sales would be paying rent to the entity that owns the building and land, just as it would if it secured a business location with someone else. Rental income is considered passive income. Passive income is not subject to self-employment tax because the rent that is being received is not based on your personal services, it is based on the value of your property. Let's break it down entity by entity.

*General Partnership*

Since the rental activity is passive and therefore not subject to self-employment taxes, the major negative tax implication of a general partnership is avoided. Remember, a general partnership will pay the full 15.3 percent self-employment tax on all earned income. Here, you have no earned income. The rental income would be considered passive. Therefore, I don't see any major negative tax problems with a general partnership. However, a general partner has unlimited liability. There is no distinction between business assets and personal assets. Owning rental real estate does have liability concerns. Therefore, a general partnership would not be my choice of entity.

## Limited Partnership

A limited partnership is not going to be my choice either. Remember, a limited partner can have no activity or management responsibilities. This could create a problem that is easily solved by utilizing another entity.

## C Corporation

As stated earlier, a C corporation pays its own tax and has its own tax bracket. It is not a pass-through entity. This creates a major problem with a rental activity. As profits are made, you most likely will want to direct at least a portion of those profits to yourself. That is why you are in business in the first place. However, how will you pay yourself? You can't just have your C corporation pay you passive income. Most likely, the money you take personally would be considered earned income and subject to the additional taxes. In this situation you have created a way to turn passive income into earned income. That is backward. I would not run the rental activity through a C corporation.

## S Corporation

An S corporation is ideal for business activities whose profits would be classified as earned income. However, rental income is passive and not subject to the self-employment tax. The big tax advantage of an S corporation is the ability to reduce self-employment taxes. Here, you don't have any self-employment tax. Therefore, I don't believe that an S corporation is the best entity for a rental operation.

## Limited Liability Company

An LLC gives you the asset protection that you would want in a real estate business activity. The major tax disadvantage of an LLC is the fact that full 15.3 percent self-employment tax is due on all *earned* income. However, in a rental activity we have no earned income. Therefore, the passive income you would earn eliminates the negative of an LLC. Passive income is not subject to self-employment tax. Therefore, I would want to own and rent the building and land through an LLC.

So, you now have two different entities running two different revenue building and wealth creating activities. Your S corporation is in the business of selling golf clubs to the public. Your LLC is in the business of owning and renting real property. You have two different asset protection plans in place and you are generating tax benefits in both entities.

Now that you have two business operations, you can focus on other tax reducing strategies to lower the overall taxes you have to pay. For example, you could set up a retirement plan within your S corporation. This will enable you to defer up to $44,000 in income per employee. That's significant tax savings. You could employ your children to do miscellaneous jobs for your business. This is a tax deduction to you and most likely not taxable to them. You could accelerate depreciation on assets that you purchase for your business. Currently, under Section 179 of the tax code, you can write off up to $108,000 of assets purchased and placed in service during the year. Company vehicles, cell phones, insurance plans, and other items, can all be creative ways to create your own tax MESS. By doing so, you position yourself to take advantage of enormous savings typically available only to the wealthy.

## CONCLUSION

Different types of activities call for different types of structures. This is a very simple example that we have made somewhat complex. However, remember that the time, effort, and energy you spend in creating your tax MESS can save you a lot of money. Over the years, this money can equate to enough to pay for your children's college educations, provide for a comfortable retirement, or enable you to accomplish things that you could not have done otherwise. Taking the time to learn how to properly structure yourself for maximum tax savings is not something that costs, it pays.

# II

## LAWSUIT PROTECTION SECRETS OF THE WEALTHY

# 6

---

# WHAT ARE THE ODDS OF
# YOUR BEING SUED?

In Part I we learned about the first component of your asset security system—Tax Reduction—and how to structure your personal and business assets for maximum tax minimization. In Part II, we'll be discussing the next component of a complete asset security system: *Asset Protection Planning*. In the Introduction to this book, we spoke briefly about what it means to protect your assets so that you can accumulate wealth. Asset protection is the area of law dealing with the structuring of your assets, prior to a lawsuit, so that these assets are protected to the maximum amount allowed by law in the event that you are sued. While many think that asset protection is a new area of the law, that really isn't the case. Throughout the history of our country, wealthy industrial families such as the Vanderbilts and duPonts and corporations such as IBM have structured their assets in such a way as to shield them from potential judgment creditors. What is new about asset protection law is that in recent years these same strategies have been used to protect ordinary individuals and small businesses from the same types of dangers. Since plaintiff's attorneys are filing equal opportunity lawsuits, it only makes sense that you have equal access to the strategies of the wealthy for safeguarding your assets.

## Who Is Zeroing In on Your Wealth?

Now that we know what asset protection is, it seems only logical to ask from whom we are protecting our assets? When it comes to asset protection, we are primarily protecting our assets from potential judgment creditors resulting from unscrupulous individuals setting their sights on our hard-earned assets with frivolous lawsuits and those lawyers who represent them. Notice that I did not say legitimate creditors. I'll be the first to state that if you've legitimately incurred a debt, you should be responsible for that debt and this book will not help you evade your rightful creditors.

But legitimate creditors aside, there are plenty of frivolous lawsuits out there that you should worry about. A *frivolous* lawsuit is basically a legal action instigated with no basis in law or fact. In some states, a lawsuit is defined as frivolous when the circumstances surrounding the suit show that it was brought in bad faith, meaning without a legitimate basis. Remember in the Introduction to this book I spoke about the common misconception that only people who have accumulated wealth should worry about installing an asset security system? I've found that this misconception is probably greatest when it comes to frivolous lawsuits.

## Are Your Assets in Someone's Sights?

While everyone is at risk of being the defendant in a frivolous lawsuit, you must understand how important it is to set up your asset security system to defend against such suits *before* you start to accumulate wealth. Why is that? I sometimes explain things using sports analogies, so let's talk about basketball for a second. Every year there are certain teams, such as the Duke Blue Devils or the Tennessee Lady Volunteers, that seem to become everyone's favorite target. Why? Because they are successful. By contrast, there are other teams, and

I won't mention any names, that opposing teams aren't motivated against because these teams are perceived as being unsuccessful. Yet what happens when these historically unsuccessful teams start to win a few games? You guessed it—opposing teams suddenly start to pay attention and put more effort into beating these teams than they would have before. Having an asset security system in place to ward off frivolous lawsuits is somewhat similar. If you are just starting a new business or beginning to accumulate wealth, most plaintiffs won't consider you a good target for their frivolous lawsuits because you don't appear to have those deep pockets that plaintiffs look for. However, that is the perfect time to begin putting your asset security system in place because as you become successful you'll appear on the radar screen of that next plaintiff trying to cash-in with a frivolous suit. By putting your security system in place *before* the threats arise, you will best protect your assets from opportunistic "plaintiffs in waiting."

In conducting asset protection seminars over the past decade, I've discovered a considerable change in the public's perception of lawsuits. In the past, many of our students would dismiss lawsuits as something that happened to "other people." Recently, people have begun to realize that lawsuits can be filed against anyone.

Are you still having any doubts as to whether or not *you* should be concerned about frivolous lawsuits? Consider these startling statistics from recent studies:

- Trial lawyers earn over $40 billion in legal fees (i.e., not judgments) from tort litigation.
- Over 15 million civil lawsuits are filed each year in the United States.
- The total cost of tort cases in the United States exceeds $200 billion annually.
- Nearly one out of every six jury awards in the United States exceeds $1 million. In many states, one out of every four jury awards exceeds $1 million.

- Over the past five years, more than 7 percent of all U.S. companies, both large and small, suffered a lawsuit costing them individually in excess of $5 million.

A great deal of the blame for this rests with contingency fee lawsuits. You can't watch television without seeing ads for law firms that are willing to work on *contingency fees*. They make promises such as "if you don't win, you don't owe us a dime," or "if you don't get paid, we don't get paid." These attorney's fees are actually contingent on whether, or on the condition that, the case is won. Attorneys will then take a portion, often 30 percent to 40 percent, of the "winnings." This arrangement seems great for people who do not want to or cannot pay upfront cash for attorneys' retainers and fees. This "no-out-of-pocket cost" is a great cover to hide the huge charges amassed by contingency fee plaintiff's attorneys. This is analogous to the proverbial wolves in sheep's clothing.

These contingency fee cases seem like a way to provide equal access to the courts when in reality they are a boon to plaintiffs' attorneys' pocket books. Attorneys can receive $750 to $3,000 an hour on average for contingency fee based cases. No wonder they are willing to take them on. They can select only the cases they know or believe will win and win big, and they can expect to earn 3 to 10 times their average hourly rate by taking these cases. From a monetary standpoint, this is a no-brainer for the attorneys. From our standpoint, you have a huge incentive to do what it takes to stay out of these attorneys' crosshairs.

Okay, that's pretty grim, but this doesn't apply to you since you don't do anything that will get you sued, right? Well, that depends. Do you own any assets? Do you have property? Do you have dependents or a spouse who owns assets or property? Are you married? Are you breathing? Not trying to be too facetious, but it is nearly that bad. In reality, one in every four Americans will be sued this year. Whether those lawsuits are successful or not, we have to expend the time, effort, energy, and money to defend ourselves against them. In addition, an

American citizen on average can expect to be sued five times in his or her lifetime. Of these five lawsuits, one on average will be what is known as a "devastating" lawsuit. Not that any lawsuit is fun and games compared to others, but the term *devastating* refers to the fact that this lawsuit completely wipes someone out financially, costing him nearly everything he owns and has worked to build.

So, do I have your attention yet? Needless to say, the odds are not favorable to you in this situation. As you can see, there is a reason why you see so many advertisements for personal injury attorneys on television—*money*.

## What Makes You a Target?

Now that we've established that your hard-earned wealth is in jeopardy, what should you do about it? Well, that's where your asset security system comes into play. Before you can adequately understand how such a realm of protection can be installed, we first must understand how it is that plaintiffs with frivolous lawsuits pick out their targets. As the Chinese philosopher Sun Tzu once said many years ago, "If you know the enemy and know yourself, you need not fear the result of a hundred battles."

The first, and probably most important, factor considered by plaintiffs when picking a target for a lawsuit is whether there are any *deep pockets* to go after. In the world of frivolous lawsuits, deep pockets refers to a defendant with sizeable wealth. If a potential defendant has assets, or is even thought to have assets, then there is a good possibility that they'll be sued at least once over the course of their lifetime. This can be especially dangerous since many people don't consider themselves in that category. You'd be surprised at what might be considered deep pockets.

When we're talking about deep pockets, what we're really getting at is: Are you worth being sued? To determine this, the potential plaintiff's attorney, before he or she agrees to take the case, is going to do some preliminary investigations into your financial history. First and foremost, county records will be checked to determine if you own any property, and if so, how much. In most, if not all counties, a property search will disclose how much a parcel of property is worth, when it was purchased, and the amount of any outstanding liens or mortgages on the property. The next thing the potential plaintiff's attorney, or his or her investigator, will do is check your name at the Department of Motor Vehicles to see what (and what types of) vehicles you may own. What do you think they'll do if it turns out that you own one or more luxury vehicles? Next your credit history will be reviewed. Such a report can provide a vast amount of information concerning your assets and, in some cases, even the name of your bank. In short, by conducting these simple investigations, and potentially many more, a persistent plaintiff's attorney can determine whether he feels that you're worth his time and effort. Be forewarned, just because you may not believe that you're worth suing does not mean that someone else will feel the same.

## How Open to Attack Are You?

After determining whether a potential defendant has any assets, the next consideration is whether those assets can be *reached*. By reached, I mean can the potential plaintiff actually get his hands on these assets in the event that he is successful in obtaining a judgment. If a plaintiff isn't able to get his hands on the defendant's assets, it's as good as the defendant not having any assets in the first place. The first consideration in determining whether a potential defendant's assets can be reached is by checking any Uniform Commercial Code (UCC) statements on file with the Secretary of State's Office to see if any present liens can be defeated by claiming that they would be of a lesser priority than a judgment lien. Another way to determine if a defendant's assets can be reached is to check with the local bankruptcy court to see if a bankruptcy petition has been filed. A third factor that a plaintiff's attorney will look for is to see if a potential defendant has structured his or her assets in such a way as to take advantage of exemptions, corporate laws, irrevocable trusts, and so forth—that is, is there an asset protection plan in place?

## WHAT ARE EXEMPTIONS AND HOW CAN THEY HELP GUARD YOUR ASSETS?

When discussing whether assets can be reached, a consideration that attorneys will make, in addition to those I just mentioned, is whether those assets are covered by any *exemptions*. An exemption is simply a law stating that certain types of assets are untouchable and cannot be reached by potential judgment creditors (plaintiffs). The most common type of exemption is the *homestead exemption*. This means that if sued by creditors, or in the event of a bankruptcy, your home is protected up to a certain dollar amount. As you might guess, the homestead exemption, like all exemptions, was carved into the law out of a concern for public policy, which in this case would be to save someone who is facing a large judgment debt from being left homeless and on the streets. The exact amount of the homestead exemption varies in every state. Determining your state's homestead exemption is an important part of any asset protection plan.

Besides the homestead exemption, other types of exemptions include:

- Retirement plan exemptions
- Wage exemptions
- Annuity exemptions
- Tools of the trade exemptions (like tools, computers, books, etc.)
- Household goods exemptions
- State-specific exemptions (check with your lawyer for these)

Can you think of the public policy reasons for each of these exemptions?

Now that we've identified what an exemption is, let's take a minute to describe how to make use of exemptions to make it difficult for judgment creditors to reach exempted assets, which in turn makes a potential defendant less attractive. Essentially, the goal is two-fold: First, you want to identify which assets you already have that qualify for an exemption and retain ownership of those assets in a way that takes full advantage of the exemption. A classic example of this is keeping your home in your personal name or the name of a trust to take advantage of the homestead exemption. A common mistake that people often make is transferring ownership of their home into a corporation or other business entity. While this may seem attractive from a limited liability standpoint, keep in mind that exemptions are only available for individuals. By moving a home into a business entity, you can lose your homestead exemption. Not only that, the loss of valuable tax benefits can make this transfer quite costly.

The second step in taking advantage of exemptions, and one that is a bit more complex, is to convert assets that do not qualify for an exemption into assets that do. The most common example of this strategy is to liquidate nonexempt assets and invest that money into a home or other type of exempted asset from the list of previous exemptions. *Caution:* The rules on such transfers/conversions of assets are extremely state-specific, so you should always consult with an attorney whenever you attempt to transfer/convert assets to make use of exemptions.

## If They Can't Find It, They Can't Take It

The third consideration in determining whether a potential defendant is worth being sued is whether or not his or her assets can be readily identified and located. This consideration is more or less an extension of the previous two we've discussed thus far. It's one thing to know what assets a potential defendant has and whether they can be reached in the event that a judgment is obtained, but whether these assets and their ownership can be found is an entirely different matter. If a plaintiff is successful in obtaining a judgment, he or she is sometimes able to force the defendant to disclose the whereabouts of his or her assets, but even then there are no guarantees. This type of asset protection planning can work well but should be approached cautiously so that you do not run afoul of the fraudulent transfer and conveyance laws we discuss later.

The next consideration that a plaintiff's attorney will look at before agreeing to sue a defendant is to estimate the likelihood that the defendant will settle out of court. Often a defendant will decide to settle a lawsuit, even one that he or she feels is without merit, to save the time, effort, energy, and money it takes to defend the suit. Think about the effect that a moderate-sized lawsuit can have on a small business in terms of time and effort. If a small business owner and their employees have to aid their attorney in answering discovery questions, give sworn depositions, track down relevant documentation, appear at pretrial hearings, and so forth, there will be little time left to actually run the business. With respect to money, even when faced with a lawsuit that a defendant and his attorney are confident they can win, the legal costs in defending such a suit can easily run into the hundreds of thousands of dollars. Another consideration that will often induce an innocent defendant to settle a worthless lawsuit is to keep her name and the name of her business out of the papers. As you probably know, the media loves to spread salacious stories, but you rarely hear about a wrongfully sued defendant prevailing in a frivolous lawsuit. Reputations are often ruined purely from news of a lawsuit regardless of whether it has merit.

I recently had a client who had a customer request a refund because the customer heard that my client was being sued. No questions were asked. My client's side of the story was neither requested nor allowed. The simple fact that this customer heard about a lawsuit caused him to work to distance himself from my client. While this is certainly unreasonable and irrational, it's a sad reality of the way some people choose to react.

Earlier, I mentioned discovery, and I think we should take a minute here to discuss what this means. *Discovery* is the legal process by which both sides in a case exchange information in the interests of judicial fairness and expediency. This is accomplished by written questions called *interrogatories*, written requests for physical evidence called *requests for production*, and *depositions*. As any party to a lawsuit knows, the process of discovery is anything but expedient and, for the defendant, it can be quite time consuming and costly. Instead of promoting judicial fairness, discovery is often used as a sword to beat down an opponent in hopes that he will either run out of the will to keep defending the suit, spend all his money on attorney's fees, or both. A properly implemented asset protection plan can cause potential plaintiffs to look elsewhere rather than to take their chances with someone who is protected.

Amazingly, the final consideration when contemplating whether to bring a lawsuit is whether the plaintiff can win. The factors considered in this decision are the facts of the case, whether the plaintiff is sympathetic, whether the laws in the state where the lawsuit is being brought favor the plaintiff's case, and whether a lawsuit-friendly jury can be empanelled. Some states, such as Mississippi, are notorious for handing down unreasonably high verdicts. Attorneys will often engage in *forum shopping* whereby they choose where to file a lawsuit based on the likelihood of a large verdict. It's a sad thought to think that in American jurisprudence the last factor to be considered before filing a lawsuit is whether the case can actually be won, but unfortunately that is where we find ourselves today.

In conclusion, now that we've discussed how potential judgment creditors, that is plaintiffs, identify their targets, do you feel a little exposed? If you don't already have some sort of asset protection plan in place, you should implement a plan immediately. According to a 2003 survey printed in the *Wall Street Journal*, 65 percent of all millionaires in the United States have no asset protection plan. Despite having a lot to lose, many people procrastinate when it comes to implementing their plan. Remember, it's too late to decide to implement some type of asset protection system *after* you are sued.

At my seminars, I often ask the question: "When is the time to have a plan, before it's too late or after it's too late?" As I look out at the audience and observe rolling eyes and snickers, I ask a follow up question: "When do most people get burglar alarms?" Now the looks on the audience members' faces change a bit. Remarkably, most people take action *after* catastrophe strikes. Don't let this happen to you when it comes to your asset protection plan. You've worked far too hard building up your assets to lose them to some opportunistic plaintiff. Activating your asset security system can keep that from happening.

# 7

---

# BUSINESS ENTITIES THAT
# WILL LEGALLY KEEP YOUR
# ASSETS INVISIBLE,
# UNTOUCHABLE, AND
# OUT OF REACH

In Chapter 6, we identified why an asset security system is crucial to your financial safety and we talked about the processes that potential plaintiffs and judgment creditors go through when identifying targets and searching for assets. We also discussed the ways that judgment creditors aggressively pursue and confiscate your hard-earned assets once a sympathetic jury has ruled in their favor.

In this chapter, we discuss what you would ordinarily think of whenever you hear the term *asset protection*, using available laws concerning business entities to shield your personal assets from lawsuits. After discussing business entities, we'll talk about exemptions and how the law already provides a shield for many assets that you may not even realize.

## WHAT IS A BUSINESS ENTITY?

What exactly is a *business entity?* While the legal definition might bore you endlessly, for our purposes, a business entity is any method of ownership and organization by which a for-profit endeavor is conducted. (Not-for-profit organizations and charities can be held in a business entity, such as a corporation, but that is outside the scope of this book.) In our discussion of business entities, we'll be looking at the following:

- Sole proprietorships
- Partnerships
- C corporations
- S corporations
- Limited liability companies
- Limited partnerships

For each of these business entities, we discuss what each one is, along with its pros and cons. We'll also touch on the tax implications of each type of business entity and what types of endeavors each type is best suited for.

## WHICH ENTITY IS THE BEST?

If you are already conducting a business of some sort and you want to eagerly start to turn the pages of this chapter looking for a discussion on what type of business entity is best, you may be disappointed. I certainly don't mean to discourage you from reading further, quite the opposite. I say this because no business entity is perfect. I'd love to be able to tell you exactly what type of entity you need, but I don't believe that's possible. Different situations call for different structures. In my business as well as in my law practice, I assist clients with structuring their assets in the best possible way for their particular situation.

The information in this chapter provides you with the knowledge to better choose your business structure.

Asset protection involves a whole list of issues and priorities. You've already seen that my concept of asset protection is somewhat different. My approach to asset protection addresses all three of the dangerous areas: lawsuits, income taxes, and death taxes. Only you can decide which of these areas is most important to you. A variety of business entities will give you the same protection from creditors, but selecting the right entity that will also let you take full advantage of tax reduction and estate planning issues is the goal. This book enables you to do just that. As I tell my legal clients: My job is to provide you with all the information necessary so that you can decide which strategy is best for your particular situation.

### Sole Proprietorships—A Plaintiff's Best Friend, Your Worst Enemy!

Let's dive into our discussion of the various types of business entities. The most popular type of business entity is the sole proprietorship. Usually, sole proprietorships are small businesses with just one owner. Unless a business is specifically formed as a distinct legal entity such as a corporation or a limited liability company, it will be a sole proprietorship *by default*. That means that you are *automatically* a sole proprietorship unless you take action to become otherwise. If you're currently operating a business as a sole proprietorship, you've probably saved a little bit of time and a little bit of expense by not operating as some other type of business entity. However, you've also been exposing yourself, *personally*, to a whole lot of potential devastation.

Before I scare you to death, let's look on the bright side of your sole proprietorship. One of the biggest advantages of operating a business as a sole proprietor is that it does not require that the business owner comply with statutory requirements regarding decision making. Sole proprietorships are also simple and inexpensive to establish and maintain. To operate a sole proprietorship, you do not have to form the entity with the Secretary of State or file any annual reports. Additionally, sole proprietorships are taxed as individuals on the owner's personal tax returns. If you just start a business but don't establish it as some type of formal entity, the business will be a sole proprietorship if there is just one owner.

While this type of option may seem desirable at first, you'll never hear me recommend a sole proprietorship to *anyone*. This may sound ridiculous, but I wouldn't even let my daughters open up a lemonade stand at the corner of our yard as a sole proprietorship. Don't get me wrong—I love my daughters and they are talented, good-looking, and smart—just like their father. But since I can't vouch that their lemonade is 100 percent safe and that all of their customers will be 100 percent satisfied, I'm not about to put any of my family's assets at risk. A sole proprietorship offers *zero asset protection benefits whatsoever*. This means that the business owner is *personally responsible for any debts or liabilities of the business*. In the event your sole proprietorship is faced with a judgment or other debt that it cannot afford to pay, the holder of that judgment or debt can look to you, personally, for satisfaction. This prohibits you from keeping your business and personal assets separated for asset protection purposes. With a sole proprietorship you've basically put all your eggs in one basket.

Let me make this abundantly clear: from an asset protection standpoint, you do not ever, ever want to operate *any* type of business as a sole proprietorship. Sure, they are simple to establish and maintain, but the risks vastly outweigh the conveniences. Don't fall into the trap of believing that you're saving money by not establishing a structure with limited liability protection. It may be much more expensive in the long run.

## PARTNERSHIPS—DEALING WITH THE DEVIL!

Similar to a sole proprietorship is the general partnership. It is basically a sole proprietorship with more than one owner. This means that if you and a partner are operating a business and you have not filed to specifically designate your business as some other type of entity, you are running a partnership by default. Unless some sort of partnership agreement has been drafted (which usually isn't the case), each owner has the right to share equally in the management of the partnership.

The advantages of operating as a partnership are the same as a sole proprietorship. There are no laws requiring that the partnership comply with statutory requirements regarding decision making. Partnerships are also simple and inexpensive to set up and maintain because, basically, there is really nothing to do outside of the normal accounting procedures you would do for any other business. Since a business with more than one owner is by default a partnership, you do not have to form the entity with the Secretary of State or file any annual reports. As you learned in the tax section, partnerships are taxed as *pass-through* entities, which means that the profits or losses of the partners are passed on to them personally, usually in accordance with their respective contributions to the partnership. That's the good news.

The bad news is that, like a sole proprietorship, any creditors of the general partnership can come after the owners, individually, for satisfaction of any partnership debts or obligations. If that isn't bad enough, the creditor(s) can *elect which owner to pursue*. In other words, if the partnership owes a debt it cannot pay, and only one of the partners has any assets, then the creditor can elect to pursue that partner for 100 percent of the debt, regardless of which partner actually decided to incur the debt. This makes it even worse than a sole proprietorship when it comes to asset protection. Because a general partnership offers zero asset protection benefits, you'll never hear me recommend this type of entity either.

Before moving on to the other business entities, let me make one final point that you probably won't learn anywhere else: Whatever your desires are regarding ownership, control, taxation, attracting investors, and so on, whenever you open a business, whether alone or with a partner(s), you will be able to achieve all of these goals, and more, with one of the remaining types of business entities. If anyone tells you that in order to structure your business the way you want you'll have to set up a sole proprietorship or a partnership, they are just flat wrong.

## Corporations—Protect Yourself Like the Big Boys Do

The next type of entity that we discuss is the corporation. You may remember at the beginning of Part II, I said that the area of law known as asset protection isn't really new, it's just that old practices that were usually thought of as being only for the rich and famous are now being taken advantage of by ordinary people like you and me. Incorporating your business is a perfect example. No longer do corporations have to be huge international companies like IBM or Standard Oil—today you can incorporate your business and take advantage of the corporate laws in your state just like the big boys do.

So, what is a corporation? First, let me bore you with the proper definition: A corporation is an entity with a legal existence that is separate and distinct from its owners (shareholders). In layman's terms, it's simply a legal "person" that you create. Is that a little clearer? Have you ever received a bill in the mail, or taken out a loan, or worse, been served with a lawsuit, and wished that someone else's name was on the paperwork? Well, with a corporation you have that option. Like any other individual, a corporation is considered and treated by law as a separate "person" for legal and tax purposes.

You're probably wondering to yourself right now what a corporation can legally do, and the answer is *anything* (as long as it is legal). A corporation can file its own tax returns, receive a loan, make loans to others, build and apply for credit, own property, operate a business, solicit customers, or anything else so long as it is legal. And how about this: A corporation never dies! A corporation is generally in existence perpetually until either affirmative action is taken to dissolve the corporation or until the corporation is dissolved by operation of law for failure to properly maintain its existence (i.e., by failing to file annual reports or take other statutorily required actions).

As you can already tell, I'm pretty big on corporations. In terms of asset protection benefits, probably the biggest advantage to running your business as a corporation is that it is the only "person" who will be sued. This is because, since the corporation's debts and liabilities are its own, only it will be responsible for them. Because of the asset protection afforded a corporation, it is a popular choice for business operation. But what if someone tells you that you should operate your business as a sole proprietorship instead of a corporation because you'll want to take the expected losses of the new business on your own tax returns, and a corporation isn't a pass-through taxable entity? Well, just keep reading . . .

## Control Your Business Taxation with S Corporations

Whenever I speak of corporations, people always ask me about the difference between a C corporation and an S corporation. The primary difference is in the way each type is taxed. All corporations are automatically C corporations by default. What makes a corporation an S corporation is the filing of additional tax documents designating the corporation as such.

Regarding taxes, an S corporation is a pass-through entity. But what about S corporations and asset protection? An S corporation is still a corporation. Therefore, it is a legal entity separate and distinct from its shareholders for asset protection purposes, which means that it is *solely* responsible for its own debts and liabilities just like a C corporation.

The downside to corporations is that they are subject to initial and yearly filings with the Secretary of State and there are other formalities such as corporate records that must be kept. Most small business owners can keep up with these requirements on their own. Also, with the initial and annual corporate filings there are fees that will vary anywhere from nominal amounts ($50 to $150) up to several hundred dollars, depending on the state. Even with these downsides, the asset protection benefits you receive from a corporation are immeasurable.

## With Limited Partnerships You Can Be in Control

The next business entity is the *limited partnership* (LP). Like corporations, a limited partnership is a legal entity separate and distinct from its owners (the partners). You'll recall from our earlier discussion on *general* partnerships that each partner has the right to participate in the management of the partnership, and each partner is personally liable for the debts and liabilities of the partnership. This is not the case with limited partnerships. In a limited partnership, the limited partners will *not* be participating in the day-to-day activities of the partnership. Only the *general partner* will have a say in the management of the company. This sort of entity is perfect for those entrepreneurs who want to attract investors but who don't want to hand over the management or decision-making duties. Another benefit is that a limited partnership is another pass-through entity, plus, the profits and losses can be allocated *any way you want*, regardless of each partner's contribution to the limited partnership. This allows for tremendous flexibility come tax time.

So what about asset protection benefits? You may have heard that there is a price for freedom, and this is true with limited partnerships. While the general partner is the only partner with any say-so in the management and direction of the limited partnership, the general partner will be personally liable for the debts and obligations of the limited partnership. The fact that all of the limited partners (your investors) will never be personally liable for the debts and obligations of the limited partnership is a great tool for attracting investors. But what about the general partner? Let's discuss a way around this little detail that will enable you to accomplish some amazing objectives through some wealth structuring magic.

### Solving the General Partner Conundrum

As previously mentioned, limited partnerships are a great business entity to use when you are conducting an active trade or business and you want to attract investors. By using a limited partnership, your investors will each be limited partners, meaning that they won't have any authority to interfere with your decisions regarding the business. And by attracting investors by offering them limited partner status, you should not have to deal with any prickly SEC regulations and guidelines that publicly traded corporations have.

There is one major drawback to operating your business as a limited partnership. As the general partner, you receive zero asset protection benefits because the general partner(s) is always personally responsible for the debts and liabilities of the limited partnership. Can you think of a way around this problem? The answer is to use a corporation, as the general partner. This way, you can achieve the freedom of having independent authority over the management of the business, but also achieve the asset protection benefits of a corporation.

Some other typical uses of limited partnerships include:

- Doing real estate "flips" and "rehabs." By transferring most income to the limited partners, you can avoid paying self-employment taxes
- Oil and gas exploration and development
- New businesses that expect losses in the initial years and the partners want the benefit of pass-through taxation

## Limited Liability Companies — There's a New Kid in Town

The next type of business entity is the limited liability company (LLC). An LLC is a relatively new type of business entity that fits somewhere between a partnership and a corporation. Like owners of limited partnerships, LLC owners report business profits or losses on their personal income tax returns because the LLC is another type of pass-through entity. But, like corporations, an LLC is also a legal "person" that is separate and distinct from its owners, who are called *members* and own units of ownership rather than shares of stock. So, like a corporation, an LLC's debts and obligations are *solely its own*.

There are some downsides to operating your business as an LLC. Like a corporation, LLCs require initial and annual filings with the Secretary of State, along with the requisite fees, and there are other formalities which must be met each year, such as annual meetings of the members, and so forth. But again, the asset protection benefits of an LLC are absolute as long as you operate it properly, and as such, any required formalities and fees are a minor inconvenience compared to these benefits.

LLCs also make good business sense, if there is more than one owner and you want to avoid the squabbling that can sometimes break up a partnership. While all the members in an LLC will have at least a vote regarding the management of the company, every LLC must also have an *operating agreement* by which the members agree to run the business, and this operating agreement usually calls for the election of one or more *managers* who will tend to the day-to-day operation of the company, and the operating agreement should also contain provisions which can solve stalemates between the members should they occur. Of course, a partnership can have a partnership agreement that can serve to resolve differences between the partners, but such agreements are rarely put into place with general partnerships, and even if it were, a general partnership would still leave the business owners completely vulnerable to the attacks of creditors and plaintiffs.

## Exemptions—Let Uncle Sam Protect Your Assets for You

The last asset protection tool we're going to discuss in this chapter is *exemptions*. Exemptions are provided by law, but they are not business entities. An exemption is simply a law that states that certain property is untouchable and cannot be reached by potential judgment creditors/plaintiffs. The most common type of exemption is the homestead exemption that protects your home up to a specific dollar amount in the event you are subject to a judgment. Other types of exemptions include:

- Retirement plan exemptions
- Wage exemptions

- Annuity exemptions
- Tools of the trade exemptions (like tools, computers, books, etc.)
- Household goods exemptions
- State-specific exemptions (check with your lawyer for these)
- Wildcard exemptions (exemptions up to a certain amount that can be used on an asset of your choosing)

Remember that the amount of a particular exemption varies from state to state. Keep in mind that while most states have laws providing for exemptions, not all states have the same exemptions available. In some states, the amount of an available exemption depends on the status of the person seeking the exemption. For example, if a homestead exemption is being asserted, the amount of the exemption might depend upon whether the homeowner has any children.

Are exemptions available for everybody? No. Under both federal and state laws, only "natural persons" (humans) can take advantage of exemptions. Business entities such as partnerships, corporations, and limited liability companies are not eligible for exemptions. The rationale behind this is that property exemptions were designed so that families could emerge from a lawsuit, bankruptcy, or other financial emergency with the ability to stay afloat and retain their necessary possessions such as home, clothing, and food. Since a business entity such as a corporation does not technically have a "home" or need food and clothing, there has traditionally not been a reason to extend exemption status to a corporation's assets.

Now that we've identified what an exemption is, we can now begin to discuss how we would begin to craft our asset protection strategy by taking advantage of them. Essentially, the steps in taking proper advantage are two-fold: First, you want to identify which assets you already have that qualify for an exemption and retain ownership of those assets in a way that takes full advantage of the exemption. How would you find out what types of assets are exempted in your state? Probably the best way to find out this information is to ask a local attorney who specializes in debtor-creditor, bankruptcy, or asset protection law.

Another good source of information would be consumer credit counseling services located in your state. Finally, there are hundreds of web sites with information on exemptions.

The second step in taking advantage of exemptions, and one that is a bit more complex, is to convert assets that do not qualify for an exemption into assets that do. The most common example of this strategy is to liquidate nonexempt assets and invest that money into a home. *Caution:* the rules on such transfers/conversions of assets are extremely state-specific. If you own nonexempt property and are considering selling and investing the proceeds from the sale into an exempt asset, you should always consult an attorney.

## State-Specific Exemptions

Besides the main categories of exemptions already identified, many states have created exemptions that are somewhat unique. For example, in Arizona there are 100 percent exemptions for workers' compensation benefits, prostheses, and uniforms for law enforcement officers. Nevada provides for a $4,500 exemption for a miner's cabin and tools. And Oregon has exemptions for musical instruments up to a value of $600. For a list of the specific exemptions available in your state, check with a local attorney.

## If You're Going to Be Liable, Let Someone Else Pay for It

Like exemptions, the final type of asset protection entity we're going to discuss really isn't an entity at all. I'm talking about insurance. First, a word of caution: There is definitely a place in your asset protection strategy for insurance. But as we discuss in the next chapter, insurance should not, and must not, be the only weapon in your arsenal.

You'll recall that earlier in this chapter, when discussing business entities, we discussed how they are used to *avoid* liability. For example, when the owners of a corporation incur a debt in the name of the corporation, they have avoided personal liability in the event that the corporation is unable to repay the debt. By contrast, our goal when using insurance is not to avoid liability, rather, we are trying to transfer the risk associated with the liability to a third-party (the insurance company). In other words, we're not removing our name from a potential liability. Instead, we're simply removing the risk of paying for that liability from ourselves to the insurance company.

Generally speaking, there are two types of insurance policies: property policies and liability policies. *Property policies* cover damages to your own assets. Sometimes it is a stand-alone policy, such as life insurance. Other times, property policies are part of an overall policy, such as full-coverage auto insurance. You might not think of a property policy as being a part of an asset protection plan, but insurance is defined as *the transference of economic risk to a third party in exchange for consideration*. We've talked a lot in this book about losing your assets to creditors, but with asset protection strategies, we're also concerned about losing your assets—period. Suppose you are injured and sustain huge medical bills and your medical provider sues you to recoup their monies? Sure, your asset protection strategy may protect your assets, but if you owned a health insurance policy to cover those medical bills, you'd feel a lot better.

The next type of insurance is *liability policies*. A liability policy protects damages that you cause to other people's assets. These types of policies cover damages such as personal injury and property. As you would expect, this is the type of insurance policy people generally think of when they contemplate utilizing insurance in their asset protection strategy. An example of a liability policy would be a standard automobile liability policy. With this type of policy, if you are in an accident for which you are at fault and you cause personal injury or property damage to another driver, your automobile liability policy would cover that driver's damages, but not your own. For this you would need a full-coverage policy that would also contain a property policy, thus covering your own assets.

Now let's take a few minutes to discuss some different types of specific insurance policies that you might consider installing as a last defense to your asset protection plan. For each of these policies, think about whether they are property policies, liability policies, or both.

## Automobile Insurance

Whether we're talking about a business vehicle or your personal vehicle(s), everyone needs to have automobile insurance. In most states, liability auto insurance is the minimum requirement, but most lenders require that you have a full-coverage policy until your auto loan has been paid in full. Many low-end automobile insurance policies provide only $25,000 in coverage. That may seem like a lot, but with the average price of most cars today being upwards of $20,000, if you're at fault in an accident and the other driver needs medical care and their car is totaled, you're more than likely going to be on the hook, *personally*, for a substantial sum.

## Homeowner's Insurance

If you've seen any of the news reports concerning homeowners whose homes suffered substantial damage as a result of Hurricane Katrina and their battles convincing their insurance companies to honor their policies, then you know that all homeowner's insurance policies are not alike. Most policies cover only fire, wind damage, or accidents and defects causing structural damage to a home. But most homeowner's insurance policies *do not* cover flood damage. If you live in a low-lying area you might consider upgrading your policy. How you use your home can also be important in determining whether your insurance company will pay a potential claim. Are you running a small business from your home such as a daycare? If so, in most homeowner's policies there is a loophole relieving the insurance company from liability if an injury results. Again, reading your policy is *essential*.

## Small Business Policies

If you own a small business, your insurance options are limited only by how much coverage you want to pay for. An *errors and omissions* (E&O)

policy covers damages that result to a customer as a result of negligence, errors, and omissions committed by professionals such as doctors and attorneys. Similarly, a *directors and officers* (D&O) policy provides coverage for specific types of damages that result from the acts of the directors, officers, or managers of corporations and LLCs. *Cyberspace* and *data* policies cover businesses in the event of Internet or computer related damages to third-parties or their own company. Remember, in today's twenty-first century marketplace, electronic data such as customer lists, intellectual property, or software is valuable property and should be protected. *Business interruption coverage*, which can be included in a business' property policy, can help a business survive a fire or other catastrophe. Such a policy can cover lost profits or the costs of finding a replacement business location and can be a lifesaver for a business and its employees. *Fidelity insurance* can protect a business in the event of theft or other dishonest acts of an employee. Finally, businesses can purchase policies, either alone or as part of a general property policy, to cover inventory in the case of a loss or defective products that are sold and cause damage to a third party. While all of these types of small business insurance policies sound great, they typically will be full of exceptions to coverage, so they should always be read carefully.

## Umbrella Insurance Policies

In many instances, an umbrella insurance policy can be the most important policy that you or your business obtains. An umbrella policy provides supplemental insurance coverage by acting as a secondary policy in the event that a primary insurance policy has paid out its full value as a result of a claim. In other instances, an umbrella policy will cover damages for events that are explicitly excluded from a primary policy. Because an umbrella policy is a secondary policy, and thus lowering the chances that it will be needed, such policies can provide several *million* dollars worth of coverage for just several *hundred* dollars a year.

## PUTTING THE ENTITY PUZZLE TOGETHER

Now that you know the various types of entities and exemptions to protect your assets, which ones are right for you? Like I said at the beginning of this chapter, I can't make that decision for you and, furthermore, anyone who says that they can is fooling you. The first step in deciding which business entities and exemptions are best for your particular situation is having all the information. The second step in deciding which business entities and exemptions are best for you is to engage in the process of "wealth structuring" with the use of multiple entities and exemptions. What does this mean? In the next chapter, you'll see how wealthy families have blended the available tools in a way that provides some phenomenal asset protection. The best part about it is that you can take advantage of these secrets for yourself.

# 8

---

# CREATING A LEGAL
# MULTIPLE ENTITY
# STRUCTURING STRATEGY

## *An Extreme Makeover for Your Assets*

Previously, we discussed the many ways that potential plaintiffs and judgment creditors can research you and your business to find out whether it is worth their time to sue you, and if so, whether they can find, and get their hands on, your hard-earned wealth. Sadly, this snooping into your life is as much a part of preparing a lawsuit as trying the merits of the case itself. For this reason, you must put yourself and your business through a "reverse extreme makeover." If you've ever seen one of these extreme makeover television programs, you understand the concept. On the shows, they take someone (or something) who is not overly attractive and put them through their miraculous transformation process so that, by the end of the show, the person is drop-dead gorgeous. A reverse extreme makeover is pretty much the opposite of that. By the end of the reverse process, anyone looking at your situation wants to stay as far away as possible. You have to make yourself and your business as unattractive as possible to reduce the risk of being sued. Similarly, you have to make your personal and business assets as hidden and protected as possible in the event that you are the target of a suit.

So how do we achieve these goals? As we discussed previously, relying on one entity or one strategy is never enough to achieve all of your goals. You must use a legal multiple entity structuring strategy (MESS) with your assets. The way that I like to explain this is by teaching people to start with a *BASE* (blending and strategizing entities) as their foundation.

## Is Your Home Safe at the Base Level?

Like a castle that has guards, a moat, high walls, and catapults, (and maybe even a dragon) to defend itself, you have to have *multiple* layers of protection to protect your assets from potential plaintiffs and judgment creditors. Achieving multiple defenses for your assets requires a blending of different entities and different strategies for safe-guarding and securing your wealth. The best part of the BASE technique is that it uses multiple layers of protection, not just to take care of your asset protection needs, but taking into account tax reduction and estate planning as well.

### Turn Your Home into a Castle

One of the biggest misconceptions I hear about asset protection law (even from other lawyers) is that everyone should have his or her personal residence owned by a business entity such as a corporation or LLC. This is a huge mistake. I realize that this may sound counter-intuitive, but your home should always be owned by you and your spouse and held in a revocable living trust. We'll discuss the revocable living trust in detail later in this book, but for those who aren't familiar with this type of trust, keep in mind that it is used for estate planning to avoid probate and reduce estate taxes.

So why would we *not* want to have our personal residence owned by a business entity? For starters, let's think about what would happen if the business entity is sued. Since your business conducts more activities, deals with more money, and interacts with more people than you do personally, your business entity stands a greater risk of being sued than you do. Therefore, if your business entity is sued, all of its assets, which would include your personal residence, stand to be lost.

## Our Financial Shelter Is Our Tax Shelter

The second reason you should own your personal residence in a revocable living trust rather than in a business entity is because you would lose the personal deduction on your individual taxes that you would otherwise have. As you already know, the amount of interest you pay on your mortgage each year, depending on the amortization schedule, amounts to a significant deduction. Moreover, this deduction would *not* be available to your entity. Accordingly, it would not make good tax sense to place your home into a business entity.

## Down Home

The third reason why you would not want to place your home into a corporation is because you would lose the homestead exemption. As you'll recall, the homestead exemption allows for your home to be protected, *up to a certain amount*, from most types of creditors. Homestead exemptions (and all other types of exemptions) are not available to business entities. By transferring your home into a business entity, you will be losing a powerful asset protection tool.

So what benefits does placing your home into a revocable living trust give you? As we just discussed, placing your home into a revocable living trust allows you to keep the tax and exemption benefits that you personally enjoy as a homeowner. Another benefit is that it allows you to pass your home on to your heirs and beneficiaries *outside of probate* (you will understand this better when we discuss probate later in the book).

Does a revocable living trust give you any asset protection benefits? Not directly, but there are certain strategies we can use that will give us this peace of mind. First, realize that your living trust will be the owner of record of your home, and if you give your living trust a generic name such as "A California Family's Revocable Living Trust," a search of your name at the property division of the courthouse will not reflect that you own a home. This gives you a layer of privacy that makes you personally less attractive to potential plaintiffs. Second, by keeping your home out of your business entity, you retain the homestead exemption that can protect your home up to a certain amount. But what if the value of your home exceeds the amount of the homestead exemption? To protect this amount of unprotected value, you should take out a line of credit against the equity and use your home as collateral. The financial institution extending the line of credit would then place a lien on your home equal to the total amount of available credit *regardless of whether you actually choose to cash in the credit*. For example, if your home is worth $100,000 and the homestead exemption in your state is only $50,000, if you took out a line of credit in the amount of $50,000 and used your home as collateral, it would appear to anyone researching the property records that there is zero equity in your home to be reached by a potential plaintiff. If your only asset is your home, and it appears that there is no value to be reached, you may have just avoided a potential lawsuit.

## Using Debt to Your Advantage

You've probably heard the phrase "buying a liability." It generally means that no one wants to buy something that will cause him more trouble than it's worth. This is exactly what I'm talking about when I say that you should make yourself as unattractive as possible, and one of the ways we achieve this is through *debt strategy*. Now, I don't want you to go and run up a bunch of needless debt because that certainly wouldn't make much business sense. But just as we described using the *appearance of debt* to help protect your personal residence, we can use this strategy to protect commercial interests as well.

Before describing how we *create* the appearance of debt, first let's discuss how a potential plaintiff would *see* the appearance of debt. The type of debt a potential plaintiff will be able to see is a *secured debt*. Secured debt means debt for which repayment is secured by collateral. With the case of real estate, any debts that are secured by the property will be reflected by a mortgage or other type of lien on file with the property division at the courthouse where the real property is located. With personal property, that is, any property that is not real estate, debts secured by such property will be reflected by financing statements on file at the UCC Filing Division of the Secretary of State's office.

Now that we know how debt is seen, let's talk about how it is created. As with a personal residence, commercial real estate owned by your or your business can also be encumbered by taking out a line of credit against the property. Remember that homestead exemptions only apply to a personal residence, so commercial real estate will not enjoy such a benefit, thus the need for a sizable line of credit may be required to protect your commercial real estate. Obviously, if the commercial real estate is already subject to a mortgage or other lien and there is little or no equity in the property, then it will not be necessary to try and further encumber the property with another lien.

Now let's talk about your business' personal property. This includes tools, vehicles, inventory, accounts, office equipment, and so forth. Again, if these assets are already encumbered by debt, there is nothing to worry about from an asset protection standpoint. If however, your business has been especially successful and has paid off any debts it might have incurred, you can create the appearance of debt by taking out lines of credit secured by the business' personal property. Another way to create the appearance of debt is to make a loan to your business, either in your name or in the name of one of your other businesses, and have that loan secured by the business' personal property. Once again, this debt will be reflected by UCC financing statements on file at the Secretary of State's office.

Now a final word about debt: I want to reiterate that our strategy of using debt is meant to make you and your business as unattractive a defendant as possible, not that you should go out and incur a bunch of debt that you do not need. Our country is largely a nation of debtors, and I'm a big believer in living within your means. Yet as we've seen, a little bit of debt can be a good thing. So if you have a manageable low-interest debt on a particular asset, you might be better off leaving the debt on the asset even if you have the cash to pay it off. Debt can be an excellent asset protection tool, but only if you use it appropriately.

## NEVER PUT ALL YOUR EGGS INTO ONE BASKET

The heart of my BASE strategy is *blending your entities*. By blending, I'm referring to the art of integrating various entities in a way that maximizes the benefits of each entity while minimizing the perceived or potential disadvantages. By gaining access to the best parts of each entity, we can build a structure that can provide the best protection possible.

Many people mistakenly believe that as long as they operate their business in one entity, they have all the asset protection they need. This is a common mistake that nonexperts make when they try to dabble in asset protection law. Most people who know a little bit about asset protection strategies (usually just enough to be dangerous) only focus on protecting their *personal* assets. But what about *business* assets? When it comes to blending entities, we're going to assume that you've already got your personal assets protected from the debts and obligations of your business(es). Our focus now becomes how to protect your business assets from a catastrophic lawsuit to keep your ability to make money intact.

*First BASE—Keep Real Estate Separate!*

Earlier we focused on strategies to protect your personal residence. We went over these strategies because for most Americans their personal home is the single largest asset they'll ever own. Similarly, for many businesses, its commercial real estate makes up a huge percentage of its overall value. This rule applies for both commercial property (such as a factory or office building) or any investment property that a business may hold. One strategy for doing this is to keep the ownership of the real estate separate from the business entity that is engaged in transacting business. This is accomplished through the use of holding LLCs whose function it is to own property but not do anything with it. Then the business entity, such as your corporation, which needs the real estate, will simply enter into a lease agreement with the holding LLC for the use of the property. This way, if anyone sues the corporation, the real estate will not be subject to attachment by a judgment creditor because the corporation (or other operating entity) merely rents the space from a completely separate entity. This is a way to isolate assets into individual entities to insulate the assets from the liabilities associated with other legal entities. Figure 8.1 illustrates how this works.

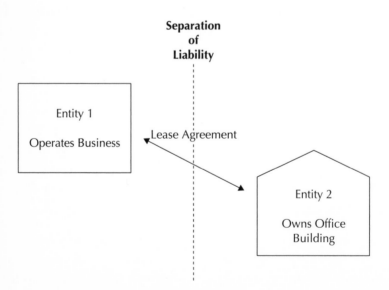

**Figure 8.1    Separation of Liability Strategy**

## Second BASE—Protect Your Twenty-First Century Goldmine

With the advent of the Internet age and its ability to be a fantastic conduit for commerce, the business world is now divided between brick-and-mortar companies (companies that have a storefront with an inventory of assets inside) and click-and-mortar e-companies that exist, and do business, primarily in cyberspace. For these e-companies, and even for some brick-and-mortar companies, their biggest asset is their *intellectual property*.

Intellectual property is made up of copyrights (books, software, or music), patents (inventions), and trademarks (symbols or logos). Why does intellectual property deserve special attention in your asset protection strategy? Suppose someone walks into a small one-room office, with no apparent assets such as vehicles, office equipment, inventory, or so forth, simply to ask for directions and they slip and fall on their way out the door. Chances are that if that person isn't actually hurt, they'll probably just get up and leave. How much could our accident victim gain by suing a simple one-room office with no assets? Now, suppose that this small one-room office is a business that just happens to hold the publishing rights to the entire catalog of the Beatles. Do you think that slip-and-fall victim will wake up tomorrow with a serious injury? Chances are he'll try to get his hands on those publishing rights with "a little help from his friends," his lawyers.

Now that we realize what a huge asset intellectual property can be, how do we protect it? Just like we held our business' real estate assets in a separate entity, so should intellectual property be held separately. Again, if your primary company is in the business of selling a form of intellectual property, such as a copyrighted book or software program you've written or developed, that book should be owned by a separate holding LLC that could then enter into a nonexclusive licensing agreement with the primary company granting it the right to publish and sell the book or software program. Suppose someone sued your primary company and got all of its assets, would it obtain ownership rights over your book? No! All the judgment creditor would receive

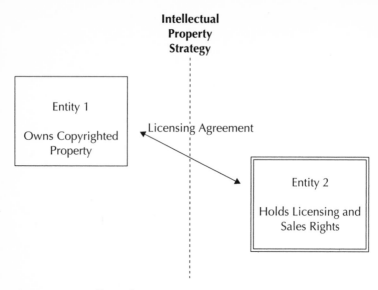

**Figure 8.2    Intellectual Property Strategy**

would be the right to publish and sell the book, and you can easily have a termination clause in the licensing agreement that would terminate the agreement in the event that the primary company lost all of its assets. The key here is that we are once again following the strategy of isolation and insulation. We're isolating individual assets into separate legal entities to insulate them from the liability associated with any other entity. The great thing about this strategy is that it works for anyone, not just for real estate (see Figure 8.2).

*Third BASE—Separate Your Trade from the Tools of the Trade*

The third step is to avoid direct ownership of the necessary tools to conduct your business in the name of that business entity. The ownership of these tools should be kept out of the name of the business itself. In many businesses such as construction companies, their primary asset is not any type of inventory but rather their construction equipment such as bulldozers, cranes, and so forth. What if your construction company simply leased all of its equipment from a separate

LLC that actually owned all of the equipment? Once again, should your construction company fall into the hands of a judgment creditor, all you would have to do is wave goodbye to the old business and start up a new business with all of your equipment ready for you to use. This strategy is often used by doctors, dentists, and other businesses with high-dollar equipment. By separating the equipment into a separate entity, we can safeguard these assets from liability associated with the operation of the trade or business.

## Home BASE—Separate the Money-Making Assets from Money Losers

Whenever discussing my BASE technique for blending and using strategies for entities, people often ask me "how many entities do I need?" My answer often confuses people, but the simple truth is that it depends on how many *money makers* you have and how many *money losers* you have. By money makers, I'm referring to assets, such as real estate or intellectual property that are either currently making money or which contain a lot of equity that can be tapped into by selling the asset. In contrast, money losers are those assets that can expose you to liability or that, if sold, would make you little or no money.

First, let's discuss the money losers. These types of assets represent the wing of your business structure that does business with the public (i.e., the one most likely to get sued) or those types of assets which have little or no value such as a parcel of real estate which is entirely mortgaged with no income or that has lost value since you purchased it. How many different entities do you need for these types of assets? Perhaps just one. If you've got five properties, and each of them has zero equity, if the entity containing those five properties gets sued and all of its assets are subjected to a judgment by a judgment creditor, what have you really lost? Nothing.

Now let's talk about your money makers. These types of assets are those that either contain little risk of exposing you to liability, are extremely valuable, and/or are free from debt. How many entities do you need for these types of assets? In a perfect world, and given our imperfect legal system, I might suggest that each of these assets be held in a separate entity. The reason for this is that you don't want to put all of your valuable eggs into one vulnerable basket. But suppose that you decide (against my advice) that your business or businesses aren't lucrative enough or attractive enough to potential plaintiffs to warrant placing each of your money makers into a separate entity. Then what is the minimum number of entities you can get away with? Only you can decide the answer to this question, but some factors to consider are:

- What percentage of your (or your business') total wealth does the asset represent?
- How much equity is in the asset?
- What are the chances that the asset will subject you or your business to a lawsuit?

Let's take a minute to look at an example using these considerations: Suppose you have three parcels of property. One is a vacant lot with no debt, the second contains an ice cream stand and is partially paid for, and the third property is entirely encumbered by debt and contains a dynamite factory. Which entity would you definitely want to separate? Obviously, even though the dynamite factory is on a lot that contains zero equity, the fact that it stands a substantial likelihood of being sued in case of an accident would warrant that asset being placed in an entirely separate entity from the other two. Remember, all assets placed within any one legal entity are subject to the obligations and liabilities of all the others in that entity. This is what makes the strategy of isolation and insulation so important and so valuable.

## CHARGING ORDERS

Another benefit to my BASE technique for safeguarding assets provides protection from *charging orders*. What is a charging order? Generally speaking, if an individual's personal assets are subject to garnishment or attachment, among these assets are the individual's ownership interest(s) in any business entities. If such interest(s) were taken by a creditor, the creditor would receive the value of the interest(s) and any rights to dividends or profits that accompany such interest(s). This attachment of the debtor's ownership interest(s) is called a charging order and it applies only to the ownership interest(s) in the business (which is considered personal property), but not in any particular asset owned by the business. Up until this point, we've been primarily concerned about protecting individuals from the debts and liabilities of a business. But now, in the case of charging orders, we will also be concerned with protecting a business from personal creditors.

## Charging Orders and Limited Partnerships

If you are considering starting a new business but you are worried about your personal creditors or the creditors of a business associate, a limited partnership (LP) will be a great source of protection. With LPs, the law in every state is such that while the creditor may reach the individual owner's ownership interest(s) in the LP, it is not able to foreclose on the interest and force a liquidation of the business. Instead, the creditor is only able to receive the right to receive profits respective to the ownership interest(s) in the LP that it holds.

Now let's look at how the law concerning charging orders and limited partnerships can lead to a terrific asset protection tool for both you and your business. Let's say that your business is held by a limited partnership, of which you are a limited partner. Suppose that a creditor then obtains a charging order against you and decides to reach the business's assets held in the LP. Can the creditor accomplish this? No. Because you are a limited partner, the creditor is not able to force a liquidation of the assets because it would gain no management rights in the LP. Even if you were a general partner, the creditor would be unable to remove you and assume the management rights over the LP because of the law concerning limited partnerships. Furthermore, the creditor is not able to demand that it receive unpaid profits. In fact, the LP can decide not to pay any profits to the partners. What can make this strategy even better from an asset protection standpoint is that even though no profits are distributed, the creditor will still have to pay income tax on its share of the profits. How long do you think a creditor is going to want to hold on to your interests in an LP when it has to pay taxes on profits it isn't receiving? Not very long. Now, this does not mean that all the money in the LP has to remain there until the creditor decides to drop the charging order. The LP is still able to conduct business and spend money on items for its ordinary and necessary operation.

## Charging Orders and Limited Liability Companies

The rule for charging orders and limited liability companies (LLCs) is a lot different than with LPs. In most states, their LLC statutes follow a "liquidation view" which means that if a member's interest(s) in an LLC are taken by a creditor, the creditor can then force a liquidation of the membership interests in order to satisfy the member's personal debt. However, in 13 states, most notably Nevada and Connecticut, the law is similar to that regarding LPs, that is, a personal creditor of a member who has taken that member's ownership interest(s) cannot force a liquidation of the LLC's assets. Understanding this concept can assist you in determining whether an LLC would work for your business or if an LP is the better option.

## Charging Orders and Corporations

When a creditor attaches a shareholder's ownership interest(s) in a corporation (shares), the creditor is able to obtain the voting rights associated with those shares. Thus, a creditor could then vote to force a liquidation of the corporation's assets to satisfy the debt. However, the law is not too concerned with this fact because the relation of a shareholder and the right to manage a corporation is far removed—that is, shareholders do not automatically gain the right to manage the corporation but only to vote on proposed actions. This is something that should be considered during the initial establishment phase of your corporation.

## OWN NOTHING, BUT CONTROL EVERYTHING

As billionaire John D. Rockefeller once said, the key to succeeding in business is to "own nothing but control everything," and this pretty well sums up my BASE strategy for both you and your business to properly structure your assets. The odds of you or your business (or both) being the subject of a lawsuit at some point are pretty good, and potential plaintiffs are finding more and more creative ways to get their hands on your wealth. To protect your assets, you've got to come up with new ways to blend your entities and new strategies for using all of the asset protection tools at your disposal, including entities, to make sure that both your personal and business assets are as protected as possible. By creating a legal MESS, you can keep yourself out of a legal mess resulting from a catastrophic lawsuit.

# 9

---

# HOW THE RICH AVOID
# MINES THAT CAN PIERCE
# YOUR ARMOR

In the last two chapters, we talked about the different types of
business entities at your disposal and how to properly blend them
together in structuring your wealth protection plan. As you've read, a
*blending* of different types of entities is crucial in fully protecting yourself and your assets. Just because you've formed your entities does not
mean that you can simply forget about them and assume that they will
always automatically serve your asset protection needs. You must learn
how to properly *operate* your entities on an ongoing basis.

In this chapter, we talk about *operating* your entities so that they
can continue to serve as the armor around your assets. This involves
three critical issues that, if not properly addressed, can cost you the
asset protection benefits you've worked so hard to achieve: corporate
maintenance, avoid piercing of the corporate veil, and avoiding
fraudulent transfers.

## Corporate Maintenance

All corporations, limited liability companies (LLCs), and limited partnerships (LPs), regardless of size, must regularly keep up with their corporate maintenance. Corporate maintenance refers to three general obligations that every business entity must perform on a regular and ongoing basis to comply with applicable laws: corporate formation, recording of annual business decisions, and annual filings. The proper handling of these matters is what I refer to as your *corporate wealth maintenance plan*.

### Corporate Formation

The first obligation of corporate maintenance relates to initial corporate formation. This is the one area of corporate maintenance that most small business entities follow, at least in part. Initial corporate formation involves deciding which entity best suits you or your business; choosing an available name for your new business entity; selecting the state where your new entity should be formed; and then actually filing the articles of incorporation, formation, or certification with the appropriate state governmental entity (usually the Secretary of State). This initial corporate formation is followed by everyone who creates a new business entity. However, a common misconception is that there's nothing more to it. The initial corporate formation of your new entity also requires drafting a document that governs your entity's activities (such as bylaws, operating agreements, or partnership agreements), holding initial meetings of the owners of the entity (shareholders, members, or partners) and keeping minutes for that meeting, electing officers of the entity, issuing stock or ownership certificates, and so on. Finally, the last step in the corporate formation phase is to start keeping a binder wherein all the entity's documents, both initially and in the future, are stored. These documents will prove vital in the event of a lawsuit or audit.

## Record Annual Business Decisions

The second obligation of corporate maintenance is the keeping of minutes and other documents which relate to the *annual business of the entity*. With the exception of routine business decisions, or actions expressly or impliedly allowed in the entity's bylaws, operating agreement, or partnership agreement, all business decisions must be authorized by either the owners or officers of the entity, and these decisions must be documented. Examples of such decisions would be paying a corporate dividend (profit), changing the registered office, electing new officers, approving the financial statements, and so forth. Such documentation can take place either in the minutes of annual meetings or by resolutions voted upon and issued by the entity as the actions are authorized.

The third obligation of corporate maintenance is the *filing of annual reports, informational statements, and/or tax returns* on behalf of the entity with the appropriate governmental agencies. In almost every state, all business entities must file (along with a fee) annual filings to keep the Secretary of State's (or other state office) records up to date with the names of the current officers and registered agent of the entity. Additionally, a tax return or other tax informational document must be filed with both the state department of revenue (or other entity which collects taxes, if state taxes are assessed in that state) and the IRS. As you're undoubtedly aware, failure to make these filings and/or payments can result in serious consequences. These consequences can become even greater if you lose your liability protection.

Does corporate maintenance sound like a lot of work? It really isn't, when you consider what would happen if your entity fails to keep up with these obligations. For one thing, corporate maintenance is required by law, and the failure to respect these obligations may lead to government fines and even the dissolution (closing) of a corporation. Second, suppose your entity becomes profitable and you decide to entertain offers for its sale. The first thing any prospective buyer is going to want to look at is your corporate binder. If you haven't maintained your entity's documentation, that prospective buyer will have no confidence that he or she is truly purchasing a valuable business. Third, suppose your entity is ever audited. The first thing the auditor is going to want to see is your corporate records binder.

Large multimillion dollar corporations generally have a large staff of attorneys and accountants who keep up with their corporate maintenance every year, and even though your entity may be small, it is no less important that your entity keeps up with its corporate maintenance as well. Remember, corporate maintenance isn't just a bunch of paperwork, it keeps its officers and owners in check and it allows one to see at all times how secure its assets are. Finally, if your entity fails to keep up with corporate maintenance, you may be in danger of having the veil of protection provided by your entity lost altogether.

## Avoid Piercing of the Corporate Veil

The second issue you must be aware of is referred to as *piercing the corporate veil*. As you know by now, one of the biggest advantages to conducting your business from within a business entity is that the owners and operators of the entity enjoy broad protection from personal liability for the debts and liabilities of the business. Yet this protection is lost most frequently whenever you commingle corporate funds and personal funds, causing you to lose the corporate veil that protects your personal assets from the liabilities of the entity. Once this veil is removed, the owners, and sometimes operators, of the entity become personally liable for the debts incurred by the entity.

This legal concept of the corporate veil of protection, based on avoiding commingling personal and corporate assets, is also referred to as the "alter ego rule." A classic example of this is when a person forms a corporation, conducts no business in the corporation, and then purchases, on the corporation's credit, personal goods such as furniture, clothing, and electronics with the intent of never repaying the corporation for these goods. The corporation's creditors will be able to "pierce the corporate veil" and file a civil suit against this person individually. Plain and simple, if you want to be treated like a legal entity, you must act like a legal entity.

Generally speaking, when evaluating whether a business entity should lose its corporate veil, courts look at the following factors:

- *Corporate formalities:* This is where corporate maintenance becomes so important. A court will look to see whether the business entity was properly formed, held meetings, kept minutes, issued stock, filed annual reports with the state, and so forth. In other words, were all of the required corporate procedures followed? If not, this is a sign that the business entity was really just an alter ego for its owners/operators.
- *Unlimited individual control:* This pertains to the degree of financial interest, ownership, and control that the owners/operators of the business entity exhibited. In other words, did the operator of the corporation act as he was authorized or however he wanted? Proper corporate maintenance and keeping up with resolutions can show that the decisions of the business entity were really entity, rather than individual, decisions.
- *Personal purpose:* Did the owners/operators of the business entity use the entity's money in furtherance of the business or to advance personal spending? For example, if it can be shown that a corporation paid for its sole shareholder's new Mercedes, personal residence, and vacation to Aspen, there is a good chance that the creditor can pierce the corporate veil and hold that shareholder personally liable for the corporation's obligations.

The veil of limited liability protection can also be lost even if you keep the entity's assets separate from your own if the entity is being operated in a fraudulent manner. An example would be using a corporation to do business that is not authorized under the Articles of Incorporation. Another example would be if an officer of the corporation entered into contracts or acquires debt that was not authorized by the corporation.

If the parties that the officer conducted these transactions with had no way of knowing that the officer was not operating with the full authority of the corporation, that officer could be personally liable for those obligations or debts.

Keep in mind that when we're talking about piercing the corporate veil we are not talking solely about civil liabilities. Criminal punishments could also result from the fraudulent use of a corporation. Remember, just because you have a limited liability entity doesn't mean that you are in any way above the law. To get the protection, you must follow the rules.

## Avoiding Fraudulent Transfers

Throughout this book I've said, and will continue to say, that you should implement your wealth protection plan *before* you need it, and this rule is especially true when we're discussing asset protection. The most important reason why your asset protection strategy must be in place before you need it is the law concerning fraudulent transfers.

One of the key ingredients in putting together a proper asset protection strategy is a close consideration of how your assets are owned. This refers to the technique of placing ownership of various assets into different entities to minimize potential liability. We know that setting up an asset protection strategy is a perfectly legitimate reason for transferring ownership of assets. However, many times creditors (including plaintiffs) try to invalidate legitimate transfers to fill their pockets with assets you may have legitimately given to a family member or invested into a company. This makes it imperative that you handle these transfers properly.

So, what is a fraudulent transfer? One question I am routinely asked is, "If I get sued, can I protect all my assets by just transferring them out of my name?" My answer to this question is No! This would be a fraudulent transfer. Simply stated, a fraudulent transfer is the conveyance of an asset by one person to another (either an individual or a business entity) without adequate consideration and which is made for the purpose of delaying, hindering, or defeating the claims of a creditor. For example, Bob has received a personal loan secured by his antique gun collection. Now Bob becomes delinquent on his loan payments and the bank seeks to foreclose and force the sale of Bob's guns. Not wanting to depart with his precious collection, Bob decides to "give" them all to his brother, Howard, for his birthday, but with the understanding that after Bob's trouble with the bank is behind him, Howard will return the guns. Clearly, Bob's intent behind making the "gift" was to defeat the bank's security interest in the guns, and as such, the bank would be able to have the "gift" rescinded.

The laws regulating fraudulent transfers are a combination of common law, state law, and federal law. When viewed as a whole, fraudulent transfer provisions protect present and subsequent creditors against transfers made with the intent to hinder, delay, or defraud them in the case of a default. Fraudulent conveyance law is found in a number of sources; but for simplicity sake, we're going to mention only the two laws that are the most relevant in terms of asset protection strategies:

1. The Uniform Fraudulent Conveyance Act (UFCA) was adopted in 1918 by the National Conference of Commissioners on Uniform State Laws and is presently the law in seven states.
2. The Uniform Fraudulent Transfer Act (UFTA) has been adopted by most States and as such is the more prevalent uniform act as well as being the most recent, having been adopted by the National Conference of Commissioners in 1984, and is the law in most states. Under the UFTA, there are two types of fraudulent transfers that creditors will try to attack: actual or intentional fraud and constructive fraud.

*Actual Fraud*   Actual fraud occurs when one transfers an asset with the *actual intent* to defeat or delay his or her creditors from seeking repayment for an obligation. In most states, such intent must be proven by clear and convincing evidence: A creditor seeking to prove that a transfer constituted actual fraud has to prove either motive or intent. Most transfers are not readily publicized, so a transferor's motive or intent when making the transfer is often hard to prove.

*Constructive Fraud*   Constructive fraud is the more common type of transfer challenged by creditors. Here, the creditor may not be able to prove that the debtor had motive or intent, but he may be able to point to one or more circumstances surrounding the transfer that pointed to the debtor's intent to defeat or hinder the creditor. These types of circumstances are often referred to as "badges of fraud" because they are commonly found when a fraudulent transfer has occurred.

Examples of badges of fraud include, but are not limited to:

- The reservation by the debtor of some benefit or interest in the transferred asset.
- Whether the debtor received adequate consideration in exchange for the transfer.
- Whether the debtor had been sued or threatened with a lawsuit when the transfer was made.
- Whether the transfer was concealed from the creditor.
- Whether the debtor was insolvent, or close to being insolvent, at the time of the transfer.
- Whether the transfer was made to a close friend or family member.

This list is not all-inclusive. When trying to defeat a transfer, a creditor may point to any circumstance that he or she believes can show that the debtor was trying to hinder or defeat the creditor's interests in the transferred asset. Special emphasis is generally placed on the timing of the transfer. Remember, the burden of proof is on the creditor to prove that a transfer was fraudulent, not on the debtor to prove that the transfer was legitimate.

Despite the defenses to a claim of a fraudulent transfer by a creditor, *it is easier to stay out of trouble than to get out of trouble.* Accordingly, here are some basic rules to keep in mind when transferring assets:

- Don't conceal a transfer from a creditor who has a security interest in the asset.
- Don't make a transfer of any assets one year prior to filing bankruptcy.
- Don't remove or hide assets.
- Don't transfer all of your assets without a legally valid reason for doing so (such as estate planning).
- Don't transfer any assets shortly before or after incurring a substantial debt.
- Don't make transfers to "insider" parties such as friends or family members.
- Don't transfer an asset for less than its fair market value.
- Don't transfer assets while under the threat of a lawsuit.

## Insurance as a Last Resort

While insurance does have a place in your asset security system, it must not be your *only* line of defense. Many people mistakenly believe that they don't need an asset protection plan because they're insured. Nothing could be further from the truth. Insurance proceeds are only paid in accordance with the terms of the policy. Sure, insurance companies are in the business of accepting the risks of others, but it's on *their* terms. Think about how casinos make their money: Casinos know that some people are going to win at the tables, for example, but because far more people lose than win, at the end of the day the casino is going to show a profit. Insurance companies have a similar philosophy to making a profit: they know that some policyholders (customers) will suffer an accident for which the insurance company has to accept liability, but many more people will have accidents for which the insurance company is not responsible, or they won't have an accident at all. Think about this: Why do more people walk out of a casino as losers rather than winners? It's because the casino makes the odds, and the odds are in their favor. Now let's think about insurance policies, which are the "odds" by which the insurance companies decide to issue policies. Who writes those policies? That's right—the insurance companies, so of course, the policies are in *their* favor.

With all of this in mind, there are two main concerns about relying solely on insurance policies for your asset protection:

1. Policy limits.
2. Policy exceptions.

## Policy Limits

You should always know how much the policy will pay out in the event that a claim is filed. In many situations, it is impossible to know how much coverage you need, especially with respect to liability policies, since you don't know how much of your money a sympathetic jury might give away in the event of a lawsuit. Still, you can often tell how much coverage is too little, especially for property policies that insure damage to a specific asset that can be appraised.

## Policy Exceptions

All insurance policies are not equal, and many times the insurance company will "put the odds in its favor" by carving out endless exceptions to its policy. Accordingly, it is imperative that you know exactly what types of accidents, events, and damages the policy covers.

Just as important as the exceptions to a policy, an insurance company can be relieved of having to honor a claim if proper filing procedures are not followed. Many times a policy will specify that a claim has to be filed within a certain period of time after an accident has occurred, or if changes have occurred to the business or property covered by the policy.

Always look for whether a liability policy has a *duty to defend* clause. Such clauses state that in the event that the policyholder is sued the insurance company will provide an attorney to defend the suit.

Regardless of the type of insurance policy you have or are considering purchasing, you should always keep in mind that the policy will fulfill its role as a last defense to your asset protection system.

## WHEN YOU NEED IT, IT'S ALREADY TOO LATE

Keep in mind that asset protection planning is both legal and ethical if it takes place *before* any event has occurred that could result in a claim against you. If you've already committed an act that could result in a claim or if you've already been sued, it's too late. Any asset transfers at that time could be considered a fraud upon creditors; in which case, the law would not respect the transfers. If that happens, your attempts to move assets out of your name fail, and your creditors can seize these assets to satisfy your debts. When all is said and done, remembering the point made earlier that can help you to navigate the liability minefield: It's much easier to *stay* out of trouble than to *get* out of trouble. In asset protection planning, if you wait until it's too late to activate your asset security system, it may not just be difficult to protect your assets, it may be impossible.

# III

ESTATE AND RETIREMENT
PLANNING SECRETS OF THE
WEALTHY

# 10

---

# ESTATE PLAN OF THE RICH

## *Overcoming the Government's Efforts to Redistribute Your Family's Wealth with the Estate Planning Process*

In the wealth protection seminars we conduct, the topic that we address first, after the introduction and overview of the asset security system concept, is estate planning. As you might imagine, it's certainly not because it is the topic with the most sizzle. The reason that we start off with estate planning is because I believe that our first obligation when it comes to wealth protection, or anything else for that matter, is to our family. Estate planning is something that must be addressed sooner rather than later because it is something that *everyone* must deal with at some point. This chapter helps you understand how best to deal with the issue.

Estate planning is certainly not a new idea. Our concept of estate planning in America evolved from the English feudal system. There were strict rules and laws for passing wealth from one generation to the next and there were stiff taxes and fees on the wealth that was passed. So the wealthy began developing means to avoid paying as much of these taxes and fees as possible. Thus, estate planning strategies and techniques developed. Much has evolved in the United States since the original system, but the fundamental idea is still the same, pass as much wealth on to your heirs with as little taxation and complication as possible. What is a new concept in estate planning, however, is the idea that estate planning is for *everyone*, not just the wealthy.

One of the greatest hurdles to preserving wealth is the devastation that occurs when wealth is passed from one generation to the next. The government, along with the various laws passed to govern the distribution of wealth, poses the single greatest threat to your heirs. This makes learning and implementing the estate planning secrets of the super rich vitally important.

## Your Money, Your Choice

Estate planning is so important because it deals with passing your estate to your family and/or beneficiaries. I know that words like *estate* can seem inapplicable, but this process applies to everyone, not just the wealthy. When it comes to estate planning, you may have accumulated more assets than you think, and you may have children or dependents who rely on those assets for support. You, not the government or courts, should be able to direct those assets to the beneficiaries of your choice, and direct the care of your dependents as you see fit. By gaining a firm grasp on estate planning tools and tactics and implementing and operating your own plan, you can rest assured that all you have worked to accumulate during your lifetime will be handled the way you wish after you've passed on. In this chapter, we begin exploring the basic concepts on which your estate plan will be built.

## Estate Planning: The Answers Are in the Questions

What exactly is estate planning? For many people, estate planning means the process of drafting a will to determine who will receive their assets after their death. While this is certainly a part of estate planning, there is much more to the process. Basically, estate planning is about answering the questions of who, what, where, when, why, and how. You must formulate answers to the questions of:

- Who do you want to receive the assets of your estate when you die?
- What assets will you pass on?
- Where can you go to get assistance in accomplishing your estate planning objectives?
- When should you pass your assets?
- Why do you need a formal estate plan?
- How can you best accomplish your estate planning objectives?

The answers to these and other questions provide you with the best illustration of the estate planning process. If you can answer these questions, you will be well on your way to developing an effective estate plan.

To fully understand estate planning, you must first understand why the process is so important. The goal of estate planning is to pass as much of your wealth as possible to your heirs, beneficiaries, and whomever else you wish (i.e., charity or an alma mater) with as little difficulty and as little governmental confiscation as possible. You already know that the biggest obstacle to building wealth is our federal and state taxing authorities. Most people know that we are subject to taxes while we are alive, but to add insult to injury, some of the highest taxes we face are actually those imposed on our estates after death. To effectively combat this peril, you must have a plan.

## The Pitfalls of Not Having a Plan

Estate planning deals primarily with the transfer of assets after death. By implementing valuable strategies, this process can run very smoothly and provide for the preservation of the majority of the estate's assets. Without a properly structured estate plan, this process can get expensive. In addition to the taxes and fees, administrative expenses, funeral expenses, probate costs, accounting and legal fees, and various state surcharges for filing and paperwork can quickly reduce the estate to half its original size. On top of this, if there is insufficient cash or other liquid assets on hand to pay these costs, other assets may have to be liquidated. Without proper planning, these costs can substantially reduce the estate that you leave for your heirs. Why work your whole life to provide for your family after your death, only to leave your loved ones burdened with debts and loss due to improper or inadequate planning? By employing the strategies in this book, you can alleviate a great deal of this problem.

Too often, we believe that when we die, our estate will simply be "signed over" to our heirs just the way we left it for them, or that perhaps your estate isn't large enough or valuable enough to be taxed or go through probate courts. These can be very expensive and time-consuming misconceptions.

The unfortunate truth is that many people have these misconceptions and fail to plan their estates properly. If you fail to implement a proper estate plan, your heirs may be faced with paying enormous taxes, fees, and other costs for your estate. They may have to pay for what you may regard as "rightfully theirs." The information that follows can keep this from happening.

As with most things, the first step in estate planning is to define the goals and objectives that you want to achieve. If you don't decide where you are going from the beginning, you cannot efficiently choose how and when to get there. Before you ever visit an estate planning professional, decide how you want to distribute your estate, then the professional can more quickly and efficiently design a plan that will help you do it. By deciding to whom you want to leave your estate, you can save thousands of dollars in hourly fees paid to these professionals by making their job much easier and more efficient. Once you've defined these goals and objectives, your professional can create a detailed design or blueprint. If you can tell him where you want to go, he has a whole arsenal of estate planning tools to help you get there. He can design a plan to help you accomplish your goals. The better job you do, the better job he can do.

Failure to define your goals and objectives can get expensive in other ways as well. If you change your mind frequently in your estate planning, you will be charged for the changes. Remember, this is a plan. It has many parts that function in different ways to achieve your ultimate estate planning goals. When you change one part of the plan, you may have to change others. This can begin to add up quickly.

## Footsteps to Follow: The Estate Planning Process

Once you've made the initial decisions, there are five crucial steps to creating and maintaining your estate plan.

1. Documentation.
2. Analysis.
3. Formulation.
4. Implementation.
5. Review and revision.

Let's look at each of these steps in more detail.

### Documentation

You and your financial professional(s) should assemble a complete list of your current and future assets and liabilities. This list should include retirement plans, life insurance policies, potential future inheritances, and other assets. You will likely find that you have more assets than you think. During this stage, you should also consider the personal and financial circumstances of each member of the family or any other potential heirs. In doing this, take into account each person's past and potential behavior, age, overall health, family changes (marriage, births, divorce, deaths, etc.), financial status, and responsibility. Remember also that in this step, your goals and objectives for your estate plan should be made as clear as possible to your estate planning professional(s).

## Analysis

Any weaknesses in your current situation should be identified and addressed, and strengths should be reinforced. At this point, your financial planner should put your estate through a simulated probate to reveal into which of three transfer methods your property will fall.

This exercise will determine whether your assets will pass:

1. To your estate.
2. Outside the probate estate by reason of law (i.e., joint ownership).
3. Outside the probate estate under terms of a legal contract (i.e., death benefits or life insurance).

If the property passes to the estate, your estate planner will further classify the estate into assets that:

- Represent liquid assets (cash or its equivalent)
- Can be converted into cash
- Will be distributed to the estate's beneficiaries

If the estate owner is married, the property should further be classified into assets that:

- Qualify for the unlimited marital deduction
- Do not qualify for this deduction

An estimate should be made of all asset and property values, as well as debts, claims, and expenses of estate administration. These estimates are necessary to calculate potential estate taxes. If the estate owner is married, calculations will have to be made for two situations, one in which the estate owner dies first and then the spouse dies, or the reverse. Both calculations are important because the estate taxes may be considerably different for the two situations. By looking at various scenarios, the professional is able to give you a view of cash needed to pay debts, taxes, estate administrative costs, and to provide for your beneficiaries' daily necessities and expenses. This will also bring to light any unexpected expenses or problems that might arise.

## Formulation

All possible arrangements that can logically fulfill your goals and objectives should be considered in this step. By doing so, the best solution for each problem or situation found in the previous step can be determined. Using the three estate transfer methods mentioned earlier, the current plan and possible arrangements can be formulated and tested. Placing your property or assets into a trust might be a better solution than passing it by means of a will.

Through this testing and analysis process, potential problems and solutions can be worked out *before* the situation presents itself and a blueprint can be developed for your estate plan. You can then have a clear picture of the manner in which your survivors will be provided for after your death.

## Implementation

In this step, you must put into action the developments, solutions, strategies, and entities determined to be the best for your situation. You may have to purchase additional life insurance or prepare new wills, trusts, deeds, or contracts to put your plan into action. The first mistake people make is by not *having* a plan, the second mistake is in not *implementing* a plan. Having a plan and not putting it into action is the same as having no plan at all. Implementation is essential.

## Review and Revision

Changes in your life, such as the birth or death of a beneficiary, property or asset purchases or sales, or changes in marital status, may bring about the need for changes in your estate plan. Relatively frequent changes in the tax code and in the applicable laws also necessitate review and revision. Periodic review of your estate plan ensures that needed changes or revisions can be made with the least amount of headache. How often you do this depends on your particular situation. If your tax attorney or accountant is a member of your estate planning team, discussing your estate plan at tax preparation time can be a good rule of thumb.

The bottom line in approaching the estate planning process is to formulate and implement a plan of action. Taking care of your family is the most important aspect of any wealth protection plan. The information covered in the next couple of chapters will assist you in making that happen.

# 11

---

## How the Rich Trust Themselves to Keep Wealth in the Family and Away from the Government

No matter how much, or how little, wealth you think you have, you'll always have enough to warrant carefully setting an estate plan into place. An estate plan is more than just a will, it's an entire process dealing with multiple tools and strategies that ensure that your estate is passed to your favorite people rather than to your least favorite, Uncle Sam. In this chapter, we'll discuss in depth the two main obstacles to your estate plan: probate and estate taxes. A false belief exists that avoiding probate is something that only concerns the super wealthy. Many people mistakenly believe that avoiding probate, and estate planning in general, is important only for those who have estates large enough to worry about paying estate taxes. Similarly, many people believe that the estate tax is something only that mega-rich estates will be subject to, but again, this is incorrect.

In this chapter, we discuss in greater detail the tools available to you in implementing your total estate plan. In Part II of this book, we discussed how no single asset protection tool can accomplish all of your objectives. A blending of various tools is necessary to completely fortify your assets. Depending on the complexities of your estate, such a blending of estate planning tools is necessary to ensure that all of your estate planning goals are in place.

## There's Hell, and Then There's *Probate*

Equating Hell and probate may seem a bit extreme, until you've had the experience of going through probate. In fact, when an attorney friend of mine uses that equation, he inevitably gets asked, "Come on, is it really that bad?" His response is priceless, "Well, they both have a lot of lawyers!" So what is this legal Hell? Probate is the legal process used to resolve an individual's legal and financial affairs after his or her death. Assets and liabilities of the estate are identified. Debts are paid. Taxes are filed. Administrative fees are paid. The remaining assets, if any, are distributed to the beneficiaries of the estate as provided by a will, or without a will, in accordance with state law. The challenge is that this can be a long, tedious process.

The term *probate* doesn't just refer to a process you want your estate to avoid, it refers to the probate system as a whole. Probate is the process by which assets are gathered; applied to pay debts, taxes, and expenses of administration; and distributed to those designated as beneficiaries in the will. Who actually does all this? The *executor* or *personal representative* named in the will is responsible for navigating your estate through the probate process, and as you might imagine, the road is sometimes treacherous. The executor is held accountable by the beneficiaries for completing his or her duties and is usually monitored and/or must constantly seek approval for his or her actions from the probate court. Without question, serving as the executor for someone's will is not a fun job. In fact, thanks to the probate process, you probably wouldn't wish the job of executor on your worst enemy. Because it is such a messy job, the executor, usually an attorney, is entitled to a reasonable fee for their efforts. Depending on the size of the estate, the executor fees charged to an estate can become anything but reasonable.

Another thing you should know about probate is that it is usually quite lengthy. While probate law generally encourages or provides for partial distribution during the period of administration, things rarely work out this way. Why? Because the probate judge must generally approve every move the executor makes. Of course, the exact procedures vary from state to state, but generally speaking, the history of a probated estate looks something like this:

1. After the funeral of the decedent, a copy of the death certificate must be obtained.

2. A petition to formally open the probate process is filed with the court. With some exceptions, this petition doesn't do anything other than open up a file with the court clerk so that the real "fun" can begin. Of course, *everyone* who is named in the will (if there is one), is an heir to the decedent, or who may have an interest in the deceased's assets, must be notified that the probate process has begun.

3. State law usually requires that you publish a notice in the paper for a minimum number of weeks to notify all the interested parties that the probate process has begun.

4. Now that notice has been served, it's time for the court to approve the appointment of the executor of the will (or the administrator, if the deceased died intestate). The probate judge has to approve the appointment, and sometimes a hearing is required. If someone (like a creditor) challenges the appointment of the executor, a hearing will likely be required.

5. The executor of the will must provide the probate judge with an accounting of the estate. The court requires an accounting that

lists all the assets and debts held by the estate. This may necessitate the hiring of a certified public accountant (CPA) by the estate.

6.  Before money and/or assets may be distributed, the executor must file a petition with the Probate court for permission to begin paying off creditors of the estate. Don't forget to list all the expenses incurred in the previous steps, the attorney's fees (thus far), and the CPA's bill. The probate judge must authorize that the payments be made. Since the judge doesn't usually issue an order granting permission for the creditors to be paid on the same day the petition is filed, a lot of time may pass before an order is issued.

7.  The executor has been doing a lot of work so far (see 1 through 6) and should be entitled to compensation. First, another petition will need to be filed, this time asking the probate judge to approve the executor to pay himself or herself out of the estate. More time passes, attorney's fees add up, and the beneficiaries still haven't received anything from the will.

8.  After the creditors, executor, attorney, CPA, expenses, and court costs have been paid, the executor can file another petition seeking permission to make a partial distribution of the estate to the beneficiaries of the will. Depending on the size of the estate, the amount of the distributions per the will, and the possibility of unpaid creditors remaining, the probate judge will probably only grant the executor permission to make some of the distributions named in the will, but not all. More time will pass between the filing of this petition and the probate judge issuing an order approving the distribution. A hearing might be necessary as well.

9.  At this point, there have been a lot of creditors making claims against the estate, and a lot of money has been paid out so it's time for another accounting. Once again, the hiring of a CPA might be necessary.

10. Property taxes are due on the assets in the estate, and the estate might owe federal estate taxes depending on the size of the deceased's assets. Time for another petition to the court.
11. The probate judge is finally convinced that all the creditors have been paid and that the estate has the assets and cash necessary to make all the distributions specified in the will. Now it's time to submit a final accounting to the court and a petition to make a final distribution of the estate. More time passes, and a hearing may be necessary before the Judge issues a final order authorizing the final distributions.
12. The probate judge closes the probate process.

Believe it or not, this scenario is rather typical of what happens during the probate process. According to one report, the average amount of time for the probate process is 12 to 18 months. Of course, the larger the estate, the higher number of creditors, and the more numerous the estate's beneficiaries, the more complicated and time consuming the probate process becomes. Suddenly, that "Probate Hell" statement doesn't seem so far off the mark.

## SAVE A SEAT FOR THE TAX MAN AT YOUR FUNERAL

Despite the fact that the United States offers to everyone the opportunity to work hard and succeed, there are a lot of people out there who delight in seeing the rich and successful burdened by hard times. If you don't believe me, just ask Martha Stewart. For whatever reason, people who reach out and take advantage of the American dream are often punished for achieving their goals for themselves and their family. One such punishment is the *estate tax*.

Do you not agree with my opinion that the estate tax is a punishment for succeeding at the American dream? Consider the definition of the estate tax straight from the horse's mouth—The Internal Revenue Service (IRS): "The Estate Tax is a tax on your right to transfer property at your death." To me, this is just unbelievable. Talk about adding insult to injury! When you work hard and generate income, that income is taxed, and now thanks to the estate tax, that same income is taxed *again* whenever you try to pass on the fruits of your labor at the time of your death.

Now that we know what the estate tax is, to whom does it apply? The question of who is subject to the estate tax is a big misconception. Like probate, that misconception is that only the truly wealthy have to worry about estate taxes. From the date this book was published (2007) until 2008, the threshold amount for estate taxes is only $2 million. Why do I say "only" $2 million? As I discussed in the last chapter, you've got many more assets than you think. Plus, since most married people leave the bulk of their assets to their surviving spouse, when that spouse dies, his or her total estate is even more likely to reach the $2 million threshold.

The realization that the estate tax will apply to you is even greater when we consider what assets are included in your estate for estate tax purposes. In a word—*everything*. Everything that you own or own an interest in, with few exceptions, is included in your estate for estate tax purposes. Additionally, assets that you have control over (such as incomplete gifts or assets held in revocable trusts) are also included for estate tax purposes. Furthermore, the value of each item when determining if your estate reaches the estate tax threshold is not what you paid for it; rather, it is the asset's fair market value at the time of your death.

## TOOLS OF THE TRADE FOR ESTATE PLANNING

Now that we've discussed the problem of estate taxes and probate, let's talk about some estate planning tools. As you'll see, some of these tools can help to legally reduce, or perhaps even eliminate, those problems. As you'll also see, some of the most popular estate planning tools offer you no help whatsoever on these two obstacles and may actually make matters worse.

## *You* Will *Go to Probate*

Whenever most people think of estate planning, the first thing they think of is the basic will. A *will* is a legal document, allowed in all 50 states, that allows an individual to make certain provisions for what is to happen to his or her personal and financial affairs upon death. A will usually contains answers to the following questions:

- Who is to receive your assets?
- Who is to be the executor of your estate and distribute your estate per your instructions?
- In the case of minor children, who is to be their legal guardian?
- Who shall manage assets left to a minor child named in the will as a beneficiary?

Sounds pretty good, right? Unfortunately, a will provides zero help with estate taxes. Furthermore, if you have a will, your estate is going to probate. So, if a basic will is the sole tool in your estate planning toolbox, your beneficiaries will not be thanking you.

## *Life Insurance Lowdown*

Life insurance is another commonly used estate planning tool. Life insurance may be purchased on the life of a spouse, a child, one of several business partners, or an especially important manager ("key man" insurance), all of which is intended to provide for survivors or to ease the burden after the loss of a financial contributor. In fact, life insurance is usually a very cost-effective way of providing for your dependents in the case of the insured's death.

In most states, life insurance proceeds are usually not included in the probate of an estate. This is because the proceeds are usually paid *directly* to the named beneficiary. As such, they are never in the control of the deceased prior to his or her death. However, life insurance has no benefit when trying to avoid estate taxes because the IRS may count the proceeds in calculating estate tax. In fact, the gross value of most estates that exceed the estate tax threshold is usually bumped over the $2 million line by the value of life insurance proceeds. Many people purchase life insurance as a way to pay potential estate taxes only to find that they are now subjected to even more taxes if they fail to structure the insurance ownership properly. We'll take a look a bit later at exactly how to handle this for maximum benefit and minimum taxes.

## It's All a Matter of Trust

Other than a will, perhaps the most often used estate planning tool is a *trust*. A trust is nothing more than a contract. Simply stated, a trust is a relationship in which a person or entity (the *trustee*) holds legal title to certain property (the *trust property* or *trust corpus*), but is bound by a fiduciary duty to exercise that legal control for the benefit of one or more individuals or organizations (the *beneficiary*), who hold "beneficial" or "equitable" title. The trust is governed by the terms of the trust agreement and local law. The entity (one or more individuals, a partnership, or a corporation) that creates the trust is called variously the trustor, settlor, grantor, donor, or creator.

## The Indispensable Estate Planning Tool

A *revocable living trust* is perhaps the most useful tool to avoid the burdensome and expensive costs of probate. By definition, a revocable living trust is a trust that is created by a living person or persons (a husband and wife) and that person(s) retains the right to terminate the trust at any time. You still control the assets that you choose to place into the trust, and since it is revocable, you can terminate the living trust at any time. At the time of your death, or when both you and your spouse have died, the living trust operates to distribute (and sometimes manage) your assets per your instructions as contained in the trust agreement. This distribution of assets takes place *outside* of probate so that you can avoid the probate process and its complications.

In addition to avoiding probate, another potential benefit of a living trust is that it can help a married couple save federal estate taxes. This is accomplished by a clause in most well-written living trust agreements called an *A-B provision*. This clause means that the first spouse to die will receive an estate tax exclusion equivalent to the credit for the year in which they die. The estate tax exclusion is essentially the amount in assets that can be transferred to your heirs without estate taxes (currently $2 million for 2007 and 2008). When the second spouse dies, he or she will *also* receive an estate tax credit equivalent to that year's exclusion amount. The A-B provision means that when the first spouse dies, that spouse's separate assets are placed into a separate trust. What this accomplishes is that, for estate tax purposes, rather than the entire marital estate being calculated for estate tax purposes, each smaller individual estate is used, plus both spouses take advantage of their respective estate tax exclusion. Given the estate tax brackets, this strategy can mean *enormous* savings to the estate.

## Phenomenal Philanthropy

Although a revocable living trust is probably the most frequently used trust in estate planning, another popular trust is the *charitable remainder trust* or CRT. A charitable remainder trust serves three main purposes:

1. Benefits a charity of your choice.
2. Receives a current year tax deduction.
3. Provides an income stream for you and your spouse for life.

Let's spend just a minute on the tax benefits of a CRT: Suppose you donate property (real estate, stocks, bonds, investments, cash, etc.) to a charity through the use of the CRT. The charity will not receive the full benefit of the donated property until some future time, usually when you and your spouse pass away. You, being the tax savvy person you are, receive an income tax deduction in the year of the donation equal to the fair market value of the transferred property at the time of the donation. Under this format, you and your spouse maintain an income interest in the CRT. This means that a percentage of the income generated by the assets in the trust will be paid to you and your spouse until you die. When you and your spouse pass away, the charity would then receive the full benefits (income) generated by the trust assets.

Another popular trust used for estate planning is the *spendthrift trust*. This type of trust is established usually for the benefit of a minor child or a fiscally irresponsible adult child, or perhaps even an elderly parent who depends upon you for financial support and/or who has a difficult time managing his or her own finances. The way a spendthrift trust works is that the assets placed into the trust never become the property of the beneficiary. That beneficiary instead receives only the income from the trust, not the property of the trust itself. Another fantastic provision of the trust is that since the beneficiary can never actually receive the assets in the trust, any creditors of the beneficiary cannot reach those assets either. So, your beneficiary will be provided for, at least on an annual or monthly basis, and the assets of the trust are safeguarded.

Earlier in this chapter we discussed the role that life insurance can play in your estate plan, but pointed out that it could also potentially subject your estate to the estate tax. One way around this drawback is to establish an *irrevocable life insurance trust* (ILIT). The ILIT becomes the owner of a life insurance policy so that estate taxes are avoided by keeping the payout from the life insurance policy out of the decedents' estate. ILITs can be complex and must be done properly to avoid the estate tax issues. If an ILIT is improperly established or maintained, the life insurance policy payout could be revoked or, most likely, included in the decedent's estate and subject to taxes if it sends your estate over the year's estate tax exclusion.

## GIFTING: NOT YOUR USUAL PRESENT!

Gifting is another, frequently utilized method in estate planning. This involves giving your heirs or beneficiaries annual gifts during your lifetime to move those assets out of your taxable estate before your death. The great part about this is that it enables you to pass assets during your lifetime in a way that lowers the value of your estate so that it can avoid potential estate taxes. The downside is that when you gift something, you lose control over it. This also applies to your assets. However, we can use a bit of entity magic to overcome this obstacle through a family limited partnership.

A *family limited partnership* (FLP) is a limited partnership established in accordance with a state's partnership statute used primarily for estate planning purposes. With an FLP, all of the partners are typically members of the same family as shown in Figure 11.1.

A common FLP scenario works as follows: When the FLP is formed, the parents (through their separate corporation or LLC) will contribute assets to the FLP in exchange for all of the partnership interests. This will include a 1 percent general partner interest and the other 99 percent will be limited partner interests. Over time, the parents will gift the limited partnership interests, up to the maximum yearly gift value allowed by the IRS without incurring gift taxes, to

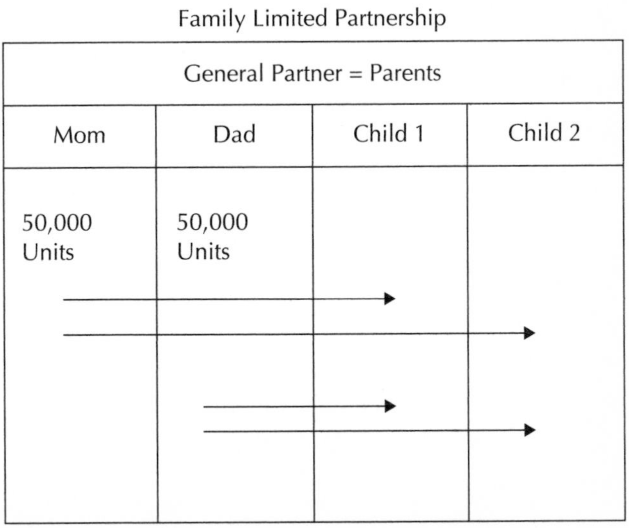

Family Limited Partnership

| General Partner = Parents | | | |
|---|---|---|---|
| Mom | Dad | Child 1 | Child 2 |
| 50,000 Units | 50,000 Units | | |

Figure 11.1   Family Limited Partnership—Gifting

their children or other heirs. As the years go by, the parents are able to give most, if not all, of the FLP interests to their heirs.

This estate planning strategy is amazing for several reasons. First, by gifting interests of the FLP to their children, parents are able to reduce their taxable estate while at the same time transferring taxable income to the children, who will typically be in a lower tax rate. This makes good tax sense. Second, since the FLP interests gifted to the heirs are only *limited* partner interests, the parents retain complete control over all of their estate in their managerial capacity as general partner. With our FLP strategy, the potential problem of a child squandering their inheritance is eliminated. Finally, thanks to an IRS strategy referred to as *valuation discounts*, the parents can sometimes increase the amount of FLP interests they can transfer to their children tax free. Valuation discounts work as follows: Suppose FLP interests are valued at $1,000 each. Any businessperson knows that regardless of the appraised value of an asset, it is truly only worth what someone is willing to pay for it. The IRS recognized this fact as well. Now consider what the "sale value" of a limited partner interest in an FLP is worth. Probably not much, given the fact that a limited partner would have no possessory or management rights to the assets in the FLP.

Because of this, the IRS will, upon request, perform a valuation discount on the individual interests of an FLP, meaning that it will value the interests at lower than the appraised value. Suppose the IRS allowed a 50 percent valuation discount of the limited partner interests in an FLP. This would then *double* the amount of interests that the parents could gift to their heirs. While this might not mean a whole lot to younger parents, older parents with sizable wealth will find this strategy to be an enormous benefit (since they have less years left to make the annual gifts) and thus can amount to a huge savings in estate taxes.

There are limits as to what you can give to each heir, each year, without taxes (currently the federal gift tax limit is $12,000). But if done properly, gifting can effectively move thousands out of your taxable estate and can give you the joy of assisting your heirs with gifts of cash or assets for expenses such as college, major purchases, grand-children, and so on.

## Other Vital Estate Planning Tools

Thanks to media coverage of the issue, most people are beginning to recognize that one thing they critically need is a *living will*. A living will is a document that outlines your health care wishes in the event that you are in an accident or suffering from a disease that renders you unable to express what treatment you do (and do not) want to receive. Not only is this document necessary so that your wishes are followed, it also saves your family from having to make the difficult decision of terminating life-sustaining treatment if it appears that you will not regain consciousness.

Like a living will, a *durable power of attorney* is necessary to ensure that your financial wishes are followed in the event that you are unable to manage your own affairs or make financial decisions on your own. Typically, when a durable power of attorney is drafted along with a comprehensive estate plan, the document will be written such that it does not become effective (i.e., "springs" into effect) until you have an accident or suffer another physical condition such that you cannot manage your own affairs.

Finally, for those of you wise enough to execute a revocable living trust, a *pour-over will* is an essential document. A pour-over will operates as sort of a catch-all that directs all of your assets to be distributed or managed pursuant to the terms of your living trust. In other words, any assets that are not specifically named in your living trust are *poured over* into the trust. While assets that are placed into a trust by operation of a pour-over will are going to be distributed or managed in accordance with the terms of the trust agreement, they will still have to be probated. Accordingly, it is still necessary to update your revocable living trust every few years even if you have executed a pour-over will.

## Some Final Thoughts on Estate Planning

Do you still think that estate planning is only something the rich should worry about? Surely not. Yet, one thing that the rich did have a monopoly on, until now, are the secrets to successful estate planning and how to pass on their assets and provide for their heirs without losing a substantial sum of their estates to probate costs and estate taxes. However, just knowing how to properly put your estate plan into place won't save your family one dime. You must *implement* your plan, and the right time to do so is *now!*

# 12

---

# WHAT THE RICH KNOW
# THAT OTHERS DON'T ABOUT
# GETTING (AND STAYING)
# WEALTHY

Many people find retirement plans to be the world's fastest cure for insomnia. In this chapter, however, we discover that retirement plans are not only exciting, but can be amazing tools for building vast amounts of wealth in a tax-deferred, and even tax-free environment. Before your eyes glaze over at the idea of struggling through an entire chapter on retirement plans, consider that besides their home, the vast majority of peoples' wealth is in their retirement plan. Over the years, this account can continue to build and even start to snowball through the miracle of compound growth. You can build exponential *wealth* through a retirement plan. Now that puts a new spin on things, doesn't it? I've been speaking about retirement planning for many years and I've found one thing that many wealthy individuals have in common is a retirement plan. To really make this point hit home, I've discovered that many people don't have a retirement plan because they are wealthy, rather they *are wealthy because of their retirement plan.*

I realize that in the early stages of your wealth-building process, other means of building wealth may seem far more exciting than retirement plans, but I consider retirement plans to be the workhorse of wealth building. The other tools of wealth building such as the stock market and real estate may be the showhorses with the glitz and glamour of a thoroughbred, but retirement plans continue to build wealth strong and steady over the long haul. Let me state my opinion about retirement plans quite clearly: If you want to be wealthy, you *must* have some sort of retirement plan in place.

But what is so magical about retirement plans? First of all, they allow your wealth to grow in a tax-deferred or even tax-free environment; second, they take advantage of the amazing miracle of compound growth. These are two incredibly powerful concepts. On their own, each of these concepts can make you fabulously wealthy. Together, they become an unstoppable force that can ensure that you achieve millionaire, if not multimillionaire, status.

## The Amazing Miracle of Compounding

When it comes to building wealth, there is nothing that will help you more than *compounding growth.* Don't just take my word for it, let's see what some of the greatest minds in history have had to say about the phenomenal power of compounding. Ben Franklin, one of our founding fathers, and a truly brilliant individual said over 200 years ago that compound interest is, "the stone that turns your lead into gold." If *Poor Richard* isn't brilliant enough for you (that would be a tough crowd, indeed), Albert Einstein supported this position when he said that compound interest is "the most powerful force on earth." While, it is great to read about what these brilliant minds thought about compounding, let's try an exercise ourselves to really help the point sink in.

## Don't Tell Me, Show Me the Money

One of my acquaintances was rather unimpressed by the whole retirement plan business. She had other investments to make and decided that retirement planning could wait. So I decided to share with her a quick illustration to demonstrate the phenomenal power of blending the miracle of compounding with the *tremendous advantage* of a tax-free growth environment. I asked her to go through an exercise about the value of compounding. Take a few minutes to try it; you won't be disappointed:

1. Take out your calculator.
2. Start with $1. Multiply it times 2. You have doubled your money once.
3. Now keep multiplying the result times 2, but count how many times you have to do that to get above the $1 million mark.
4. As you go, you will begin to get excited as you see the impact of doubling your money on the total.
5. How many times do you have to double your money to reach a $1 million total? Let's see Table 12.1.

When she was done, she called me and very excitedly couldn't wait to get started utilizing the power of compounding. However, she wasn't yet convinced as to the importance of doing this in a retirement plan.

She asked, "Can you do this in an ordinary savings or investment program?" Unfortunately, you can't get these same results from just any type of program. What most people never take the time to comprehend is that other savings and/or investment environments are subject to taxes. My friend found out just what the devastation of taxes did to her investment once I had her go through another exercise. Think taxes are no big deal? Let's look at what taxes can do to devastate this same investment scenario. The illustration that follows presumes a total tax bracket of 30 percent. As you learned earlier in the book, this is a conservative estimate.

**Table 12.1  Double Your Money**

|    | Your Money ($) | Your Money Doubled ($) |
|----|----------------|------------------------|
| 1  | 1.00 | 2.00 |
| 2  | 2.00 | 4.00 |
| 3  | 4.00 | 8.00 |
| 4  | 8.00 | 16.00 |
| 5  | 16.00 | 32.00 |
| 6  | 32.00 | 64.00 |
| 7  | 64.00 | 128.00 |
| 8  | 128.00 | 256.00 |
| 9  | 256.00 | 512.00 |
| 10 | 512.00 | 1,024.00 |
| 11 | 1,024.00 | 2,048.00 |
| 12 | 2,048.00 | 4,096.00 |
| 13 | 4,096.00 | 8,192.00 |
| 14 | 8,192.00 | 16,384.00 |
| 15 | 16,384.00 | 32,768.00 |
| 16 | 32,768.00 | 65,536.00 |
| 17 | 65,536.00 | 131,072.00 |
| 18 | 131,072.00 | 262,144.00 |
| 19 | 262,144.00 | 524,288.00 |
| 20 | 524,288.00 | 1,048,576.00 |

Begin with the same steps as the previous exercise:

1.  Take out your calculator.
2.  Start with $1. Multiply it times 2. You have doubled your money once. But now, subtract 30 percent from the gain for taxes.
3.  Now keep multiplying the result times 2, but subtract 30 percent from the gain each time for taxes.
4.  Do this the same 20 times as you did in the first exercise.
5.  After 20 times of doubling your money, then subtracting 30 percent for taxes, what is your total? Is it close to a million? Let's see Table 12.2.

Would you have guessed that total? The difference is over a million dollars. Let that sink in. This is huge! Most Americans think that

Table 12.2    The Devastating Impact of Taxes

|     | Your Money ($) | Your Money Doubled ($) | Taxes (%) | Your Money Minus Taxes ($) |
| --- | --- | --- | --- | --- |
| 1  | 1.00 | 2.00 | 30.00 | 1.70 |
| 2  | 1.70 | 3.40 | 30.00 | 2.89 |
| 3  | 2.89 | 5.78 | 30.00 | 4.91 |
| 4  | 4.91 | 9.83 | 30.00 | 8.35 |
| 5  | 8.35 | 16.70 | 30.00 | 14.20 |
| 6  | 14.20 | 28.40 | 30.00 | 24.14 |
| 7  | 24.14 | 48.28 | 30.00 | 41.03 |
| 8  | 41.03 | 82.07 | 30.00 | 69.76 |
| 9  | 69.76 | 139.52 | 30.00 | 118.59 |
| 10 | 118.59 | 237.18 | 30.00 | 201.60 |
| 11 | 201.60 | 403.20 | 30.00 | 342.72 |
| 12 | 342.72 | 685.44 | 30.00 | 582.62 |
| 13 | 582.62 | 1,165.24 | 30.00 | 990.46 |
| 14 | 990.46 | 1,980.92 | 30.00 | 1,683.78 |
| 15 | 1,683.78 | 3,367.56 | 30.00 | 2,862.42 |
| 16 | 2,862.42 | 5,724.85 | 30.00 | 4,866.12 |
| 17 | 4,866.12 | 9,732.24 | 30.00 | 8,272.40 |
| 18 | 8,272.40 | 16,544.81 | 30.00 | 14,063.08 |
| 19 | 14,063.08 | 28,126.17 | 30.00 | 23,907.24 |
| 20 | 23,907.24 | 47,814.49 | 30.00 | 40,642.31 |

being a millionaire is out of their reach. I'm here to tell you that if you start early enough or work with the right plan, *there is no reason that anyone out there doesn't have the potential to become a millionaire!* Does that get you excited? If not, then perhaps you need to take some vitamin supplements. This is amazing! The key is to combine these outrageously powerful concepts together to provide the best wealth-building mechanism available. It's called a *retirement plan.*

Even after all of this dynamic information, many people still never establish any sort of retirement plan. We know that over 25 percent of us will be sued each year, nearly all of us pay taxes, but *all* of us that reach retirement age will need the support of a properly designed retirement plan. Despite this undeniable fact, surprisingly few people tap into this magnificent money machine.

Let's look at some eye-opening statistics. An independent survey by the Employee Benefit Research Institute determined that:

> Although most financial experts estimate that retirees will need 70–80 percent of their current income to meet everyday living expenses, nearly 40 percent of all workers guess that they will need less than 70 percent of their preretirement income to live comfortably after leaving the workforce.

Okay, so we're about 10 percent off in estimation, right? No big deal. However, add this to the mix. The Economic Policy Institute responds by adding that:

> Today more than 40 percent of households headed by a person nearing retirement lack the ability to maintain even half of their current income when they retire.

Hold it. Could you live on *half* your current income during retirement? Charles Schwab, one of the biggest names in personal investments, has this to say about retirement savings:

> Individuals need to save $230,000 for every $1,000 they will need in monthly retirement income. However, only 31 percent of working Americans have saved $100,000 or more for retirement in total.

Think about this, if you currently need $2,000 a month in income ($24,000 per year), according to estimates from leading investment company Charles Schwab, you need at least $460,000 in savings. How are you doing with that?

### I've Got It Covered

Many people mistakenly believe that the government will take care of them through Social Security. Let's face it, *while we'd like to think that the money we currently contribute to the Social Security system will pay off some day, we must realize that it is highly likely that it won't*. In fact, most retirement experts predict that the Social Security fund will start losing money in 2020 and that it will be totally depleted by 2052. Should the fund run dry, projected Social Security benefits are expected to drop 20 percent to 30 percent of current payments. With inflation and the rising cost of living, this could be devastating.

But hopefully you are one of the lucky ones who has a wonderful retirement plan through your current, long-term employer and are fully vested in your retirement plan. You are set, right? I will default to the "lawyer's answer"—it depends. According to the same study by the Employee Benefit Research Institute:

Almost 7 in 10 workers (68 percent) expect to work into retirement but 4 in 10 retirees end up having to leave the workforce earlier than expected due to health problems, disability or company downsizing.

Can you guarantee your health to retirement age? Can you guarantee that you won't be injured or become disabled? Can you guarantee the "health" of your employer until retirement? If you think you can, I have one word for you that should send chills up your retirement spine: *Enron*. Even if a corporation has the best of intentions for its employees, in today's litigious society, a company can go belly up from any number of outside and inside forces and cost you your retirement savings. You must prepare yourself so that this doesn't happen to you.

## You're on Your Own

In 2006, Congress enacted legislation to protect pensions and give Americans more control over their retirement plans. As with all acts of Congress, this plan has pros and cons. One of the pros in the past was that you contributed to your retirement plan and it basically flew on autopilot. If you stayed with the company, you could hope for a relatively comfortable retirement. The biggest con was that, like the Enron fiasco, you had no control over your retirement and it was completely linked to the success or failure of your company. In response to this, Congress enacted the Pension Protection Plan of 2006. While the name sounds like a stone fortress to protect your retirement plan, the reality, as described by Charles Schwab, is this:

> The message of the Pension Protection Act: You're on your own.

You may have a fortress, but you have no reinforcements, no supplies, and no one to rely on but yourself and your team, *if you have one*. This can be incredibly exciting for some people and unbelievably terrifying for others. The difference between these two groups is their level of knowledge regarding retirement plans.

## Golden Years or Golden Arches

While your vision of retirement may include exotic travel, leisure activities, or relaxing in a rocking chair while telling stories to your grandchildren, there are other scenarios for which you must plan. In fact, if you fail to make plans for your retirement, you may find your-self destitute. On the other hand, a well-designed retirement plan will virtually guarantee that you retire comfortably and with the wealth and income you need to enjoy your retirement. I refer to the two ends of the retirement spectrum as, "Golden Years" or "Golden Arches."

By Golden Arches, you may have guessed, I mean McDonalds. Think about this, who do you see working under the Golden Arches? No offense to any fast-food restaurant, but you typically see teenagers and the elderly working there. Well, teenagers, we can understand, but do you think seniors worked all their lives and saved for their golden years to realize that they have to return to the workforce in the fast-food industry? Again, no offense, but do you think the seniors who are working at these establishments are doing so just because they *want* to?

Simply put, a good retirement plan helps ensure that you won't outlive your income. Having said that, the quality of life you live dur-ing that time depends on what you are willing to contribute *today*. I realize that "exciting" isn't a term that usually comes to mind when discussing retirement plans, but after reading about the powerful, wealth-building opportunities available through retirement plans, please realize that *you* are in control of your future. How exciting that future will be depends on you.

You control whether you have Golden Years or Golden Arches in your future, that is, whether you retire wealthy or retire with a part-time job. If this sounds harsh, this is just a taste of reality, and reality can be much harsher than anything you may have imagined.

## It's All Up to You

Besides the unreliability of Social Security and pensions, another reason why actively planning for retirement is so important is inflation. While it is a term most of us are pretty familiar with, the impact it can have on your finances is often overlooked. Inflation diminishes the purchasing power of money. In other words, as the years go by, you will pay more for the same goods and get less for the same amount of money. Inflation is one of those concepts that can mean different things to different people. While it can devastate the financial situations of the uneducated, those who understand the world of real estate investment can make fortunes through times of inflation. This underscores the importance of gaining knowledge. In the next chapter, we discuss how to conduct real estate investments within a retirement plan to catapult your finances to another level.

Perhaps the most important thing to prepare for when planning your retirement is the flexibility to deal with changes. Regardless of the unforeseen challenges you may encounter, there is much to be said for the peace of mind that a sizable nest egg can provide. Capitalism is a beautiful thing, indeed, but one thing we know is that the economy is unpredictable. So for that reason, it becomes especially important to establish the right type of plan. If you think you have waited too late to build your wealth, if you want to slash your retirement age by years or decades, or if you just want to create vast amounts of wealth as rapidly as possible, continue to read this chapter. Once we've covered the basics, you can go on to the really amazing strategies in the next chapter, where we "heat up" the retirement power planning with the hottest retirement planning methods available, self-directed retirement plans.

## FAILING TO PLAN IS PLANNING TO FAIL

Now that you know how important it is to plan for your retirement, we next need to decide which type of retirement plan will best meet your needs. To fully understand the basics of retirement plans, we specifically need to take a look at the four basic categories of such plans:

1. Individual Retirement Accounts.
2. Qualified Plans.
3. Quasi-Qualified Plans.
4. Nonqualified Plans.

While law libraries and tax codes are filled with literally thousands of laws, legal opinions, and tax regulations concerning retirement plans, you can take solace in the fact that every type of plan falls into one of these four categories. With that in mind, let's take a look at each one individually.

### Individual Retirement Accounts—Something for Everyone

An Individual Retirement Account (IRA) provides either a tax-deferred or tax-free way of saving for retirement. There are many different types of accounts within the world of IRAs, depending on the financial goals and situations of each individual. These types of IRAs include:

*Traditional Contributory Individual Retirement Accounts* Anybody who has income from a business or employment may establish and contribute to an IRA. As we mentioned earlier, the only requirement is that you have *earned income*. In other words, money that you've inherited or that you receive as a bonus or from passive investments cannot be contributed into an IRA.

Because of the tax advantages of the various IRAs, our good friends in Congress have placed limits on the amount of money we can contribute annually to an IRA. The limits depend on two things: (1) the year in which the contribution was made, and (2) the IRA participant's age.

Fortunately, the amount that we are able to contribute annually to an IRA continues to increase. After 2008, the contribution limit will increase in increments of $500 per year, depending on the level of inflation. These contribution limits apply to *all* types of IRAs, not just this first category.

Contributions and earnings are taxed when withdrawn after age 59½. Withdrawals before the age 59½ are taxable and subject to a 10 percent penalty with certain exceptions. Additionally, withdrawals must begin by the year after you reach age 70½ to avoid penalties.

We also need to look at the tax benefits of a traditional contributory IRA. If you're *not* covered by an employer's retirement plan, you may take a deduction on your tax return in the amount of your contribution. If you *are* covered by an employer's plan, then your IRA contribution may or may not be deductible depending upon your gross income.

*Rollover IRAs*   Suppose you have an employer-sponsored qualified retirement plan and you want to change jobs. If you are of retirement age and receive distributions from your IRA that you would like to reinvest, you might be a good candidate for a Rollover IRA.

A Rollover IRA is categorized separately because of the source of your contribution into the IRA. To rollover means to transfer money from a qualified retirement plan such as a 401(k) into an IRA. If you receive a payout from your company-sponsored retirement plan, a Rollover IRA could be to your advantage. It is important to note that you will continue to receive the tax-deferred status of your retirement savings and you will avoid penalties and taxes. The same age limitations, taxation, and withdrawal penalties apply to Rollover IRAs as to traditional IRAs.

*Roth IRAs*  A relatively recent development in the world of IRAs is the Roth IRA. The Roth IRA provides no tax deductions for contributions like there are with traditional contributory IRAs. A Roth IRA, however, has a potentially enormous advantage in that it provides a benefit that isn't available for any other form of retirement savings: If you meet certain requirements, all earnings are tax free when you or your beneficiary withdraw them. You read that right, *tax free*. Additionally, a Roth IRA avoids the early distribution penalty on certain withdrawals, and eliminating the need to take minimum distributions after age 70½.

The chief advantage of the Roth IRA is obvious: the ability to have investment earnings *completely* escape taxation. However, unlike traditional contributory IRAs, you get no tax deduction for your contribution to the Roth IRA.

There are just two requirements for having a Roth IRA: (1) you must have income equal to the amount contributed, and (2) your modified adjusted gross income can't exceed certain limits. The current (2007) limits are $95,000 for single individuals (or $150,000 for married individuals filing joint returns). The amount you can contribute is reduced gradually and then completely eliminated when your modified adjusted gross income exceeds $110,000 (single) or $160,000 (married filing jointly).

You can also convert a regular IRA to a Roth IRA. But two rules apply: (1) your modified adjusted gross income must be $100,000 or less, and (2) you must either be single or file your tax return jointly with your spouse. Taxes are owed in the year of the conversion, but for many people the long-term savings outweigh the conversion tax.

Which type of plan is best for you, a regular IRA or a Roth IRA? For those nearing retirement where IRA earnings are not expected to significantly increase by retirement, the immediate deductions from contributing to a traditional contributory IRA may be best. For most, especially those who have many years to save for retirement, a Roth IRA may be a better choice. Before any decisions are made, let's look at some other options.

*Simplified Employee Pension*    A simplified employee pension (SEP) is a special type of IRA that is established by an employer for the benefit of its employees or by small business owners for their own benefit. Simplified employee pensions have many of the characteristics of a qualified plan but, as the name implies, are much easier to set up and administer. Under an SEP, each participant in the plan has his or her own retirement account into which the employer contributes. These contributions are excluded from the employee's pay and are not taxable until the funds are distributed. For persons who are self-employed, an SEP can be established even if they have zero employees.

*Simple IRAs*    A simplified incentive match plan for employees, a SIMPLE IRA is designed to make it easier for small business owners to establish a retirement plan for its employees. The good thing about a SIMPLE IRA is that it is a salary reduction plan, like a 401(k), and it allows employees to divert some compensation into retirement savings.

## Qualified Plans—Safe and Sound

The next type of retirement plan is the *qualified plan*. A qualified plan is a forced savings plan that is set up by an employer to benefit its workers and is described in §401 of the U.S. Tax Code. It provides tax incentives to encourage employers to set up and contribute to such retirement plans, while at the same time, encourages employees to put some of their earnings back into the plan. The term *qualified* indicates that this type of plan is governed by the Employee Retirement Income Security Act (ERISA). This means that there are federal guidelines for how money in qualified plans is maintained. Therefore, your account is not considered an asset of your employer. Rather, it is held in trust in a separate account for you separate and apart from the company's money. Like IRAs, there are many types of qualified plans for you to choose from.

*401(k) Plans*    Perhaps the most common type of qualified plan is the 401(k). A 401(k) allows employees to save and invest for their own retirement. Through a 401(k), you can authorize your employer to deduct a certain amount of money from your paycheck before taxes are calculated and to invest that money into the 401(k) plan. Your money is placed in investment options selected through your company's plan. The great thing about contributing to a 401(k) is that contributions are made with pretax dollars. This means that you can actually lower the amount you pay each pay period in current taxes. For example, if you earn $1,000 each paycheck and you contribute, say 5 percent ($50), you are only taxed on $950. You don't owe income taxes on the money until you withdraw it from the plan, which provides for tax-free growth until retirement when you will probably be in a lower tax bracket.

*Other Qualified Plans*   Certainly, the 401(k) is not the only type of qualified plan, but from our discussion, you can see why it's the most popular. Let's take a brief look at several other types of qualified plans:

- *Stock bonus plans:* This type of qualified plan is like a typical profit-sharing plan except that, regarding the employee's distribution, the employer must pay the benefits in the form of shares of company stock.
- *Money purchase pension plan:* This type of plan is somewhat similar to the typical profit-sharing plan because the employer's contributions are allocated to each participant's individual account. The difference is that the employer's contributions are *mandatory*, not discretionary.
- *Employee stock ownership plan:* This qualified plan (also called an ESOP) is a type of stock bonus plan that may also have some features of a money purchase pension plan. The current (2007) yearly contribution limit of an ESOP is 25 percent of the participant's total compensation up to a maximum of $40,000.
- *Defined benefit plan:* This type of qualified plan is an employer-sponsored plan where employee benefits are sorted out based on a formula, using factors such as salary history and duration of

employment. Investment risk and portfolio management are entirely under the control of the company.

- *Target benefit plan:* This type of qualified plan is similar to a defined benefit plan since contributions are based on projected retirement benefits. However, unlike a defined benefit plan, the benefits provided to participants at retirement are based on the performance of the investments and are therefore not guaranteed.

- *Plans for self-employed people:* If you are self-employed or the owner of an unincorporated business, you are able to take advantage of what is commonly referred to as a Keogh plan. Money you place into a Keogh account grows tax-free until it is withdrawn subject to the age limitations mentioned earlier.

As with the 401(k), the primary advantage of qualified plans to the employee is the opportunity to take advantage of deferring taxes until distribution. That means you can postpone paying income taxes on the earnings contributed to the plan and the returns on the contribution itself until the money is taken out of the plan. Additionally, by placing the plan's assets into a trust that is generally protected from creditors, contributions are safeguarded so that they will still be there when the employee retires.

## Quasi-Qualified Plans

The next type of plan is what I refer to as "quasi-qualified." Quasi-qualified plans have many features similar to qualified plans, which is why I refer to them as "quasi-qualified." The two most common types of quasi-qualified plans are qualified annuity plans and tax-deferred annuities. These plans, also called hybrid plans, are tucked away deep in the U.S. Tax Code. Of these types of quasi-qualified plans, the two most common are qualified annuity plans and tax-deferred annuities.

*Qualified Annuity Plan*   The basic rules for qualified retirement plans state that the assets of the plan must be held by an administrator in a trust. For those of you who happen to have a copy of the U.S. Tax Code close by, turn to §403(a). This section of the Tax Code provides for an exception to the rule I just stated, and it instead allows employers to use contributions from the participants of their plans to purchase annuities directly from an insurance company. This alternative to holding contributions in a trust serves to simplify the administration of the plan. In almost every other respect, the rules for qualified annuity plans are the same as those for qualified retirement plans in general.

*Tax-Deferred Annuity*    For those of you who qualify, a type of annuity plan, commonly called a tax-deferred annuity (TDA) or 403(b) plan may be another tool for planning for retirement. These plans are usually funded from individual annuity contracts that are purchased from insurance companies. After retirement, benefits are typically paid as a monthly annuity for the duration of your life. However, some TDAs offer other distribution options upon retirement, such as lump sum payments.

## *Nonqualified Plans—Proceed with Caution*

Nonqualified retirement plans are basically special incentive and/or compensation packages that are offered to key employees. Such plans may be in the form of stock certificates, stock options, or deferred cash bonuses. Companies that offer these types of retirement plans don't have to offer lower-level employees the same type of retirement benefits that are offered to its executives. These types of retirement plans are also not subject to the same vesting, participation, and distribution requirements that the other three categories of retirement plans must generally adhere to.

There are also some other features of nonqualified plans that make it distinctive from other types of retirement plans: (1) contributions to nonqualified plans are not deductible by an employer, (2) there is no requirement that assets contributed to nonqualified plans be held in trust, and (3) perhaps the most significant distinction between nonqualified plans and other retirement plans is that the assets of the individual participants in the plan are not protected from creditors. As you know, this is not as desirable from an asset protection standpoint.

Now let's take a minute or two to talk about the tax consequences for nonqualified plans. Nonqualified plans generally allow employees to defer the taxation of part of their current compensation until later years. As I stated earlier, these nonqualified plans are used for highly paid executives, and part of the reason is because they usually have already deferred the maximum pay allowed under qualified plans, such as 401(k) plans. The basic premise behind nonqualified arrangements is that the deferred compensation is not taxable as long as there are "strings attached" to the ability of the participating employee to withdraw the deferrals. For example, these strings could include a risk of forfeiture if the employee should leave employment or if the employer should go out of business. You must take this into consideration when selecting which type of plan offers you the most bang for your buck.

## BEGIN YOUR RETIREMENT PLAN TODAY

I think you can see why I'm a big fan of retirement plans and, now that you've begun to familiarize yourself with the many types of available plans, you can better decide which plan is right for you. Because of the miracle of compounding and the tax benefits that the various plans provide, there is no reason why anyone should retire as anything other than a millionaire. These are some powerful, wealth-building tools that you can take advantage of as a part of your overall retirement plan. Now if you are really ready to kick it up a notch, the next chapter shows you how to take the retirement planning tactics and supercharge them through the use of advanced tools and strategy to build even more phenomenal wealth through your retirement plan. When selecting the plan that best suits you, remember that a retirement planning professional can best guide you through the decision-making process.

# 13

---

# TAKING CONTROL OF YOUR
# FINANCIAL FUTURE

The information contained in this chapter can make you enormously wealthy. Thanks to the miracle of compounding and the tax-free growth that retirement plans offer, *everyone* not only can, but *should* retire as a millionaire. Because of this, retirement plans are phenomenally powerful tools to enable you to spend your retirement years in style and pass on a legacy of wealth to your heirs.

By now, you've come to realize the phenomenal wealth-building benefits that a retirement plan can offer. However, you might be a little sad. Why? While it's great to be able to plan for a leisurely retirement, the amazing abilities that retirement plans have in building a nest egg are often controlled solely by the administrator of the plan. How powerful would it be if you were able to build your wealth by harnessing the amazing power of retirement plans yourself? It could be outstanding if you learn how to do it properly. The great news for you is that it is not only possible, but also entirely probable, that you can indeed take control over the quality of your retirement.

With the amazing power of retirement plans in *your hands*, you can take full advantage of the power of compounding growth in a tax-free environment. A true *self-directed retirement plan* is typically done through an IRA. This type of plan is not only a powerful wealth-building tool, but has additional asset protection and tax reduction benefits as well.

## SAFEGUARDING YOUR NEST EGG

Your financial planner may never have told you that a retirement plan could be a great asset protection tool, but it's true. A little-known fact is that most states exempt retirement accounts from the assets that can be liquidated or seized by potential plaintiffs and judgment creditors. This means that even if you are sued individually, your retirement plan should be safely protected. Therefore, using retirement plans should not only be a cornerstone of your overall financial strategy, but a key strategy for providing asset protection benefits in the event of bankruptcy or litigation by creditors.

Would you like a real-world example of how this strategy actually works? Perhaps you've heard of a former professional football player named O. J. Simpson. After being found not guilty for the murders of his ex-wife Nicole Brown Simpson and her friend Ronald Goldman in a much-publicized criminal trial, the families of the victims brought a civil action against Simpson individually. The civil suit alleged that Simpson was civilly liable for the wrongful deaths of Nicole and Ron. A jury agreed and awarded the Brown and Goldman families a total of $33.5 million dollars in damages. As any lawyer will tell you, obtaining a judgment against a defendant is one thing, but actually collecting on the judgment is another. To date, the Brown and Goldman families have received very little money from Simpson in satisfaction of the judgment.

Why is this? Despite the fact that Simpson earned millions playing football, doing commercials, and acting in movies, his primary asset is his NFL pension plan. Pension plans have been safe from creditors, including civil judgment holders, for many years. So what does this mean for you? Well, in 2005, the U.S. Supreme Court confirmed that the asset protection benefits afforded to pension plans also extend to

Individual Retirement Accounts (IRAs) and other self-directed forms of investment, in most states.

## Don't Forget about the Tax Benefits

In addition to the asset protection benefit of retirement plans, it bears repeating that one of the reasons why retirement plans are such great wealth-building tools is because of the tax treatment that they receive. As you'll recall, depending on the type of retirement plan, there are great tax-planning benefits that can legally delay or even exempt appreciation and growth from all income taxes. Better still, these favorable tax treatments are also enjoyed by self-directed retirement plans.

## What Can an IRA Own?

Before we can define and discuss self-directed retirement plans, we need to discuss what types of assets a retirement plan can own. For many people, owning a retirement plan such as an IRA or 401(k) means owning one of three basic types of investments:

1. Stocks.
2. Bonds.
3. Mutual funds owning stocks or bonds.

Why do you think that most retirement plans only hold stocks, bonds, or mutual funds? Think about who provides most private retirement plans: investment firms or large financial companies that own investment firms. What do investment firms also sell? You guessed it: stocks, bonds, and mutual funds. Since it is obviously in the best interest of investment firms that you set up your retirement plans with securities that they sell, these are typically the only types of assets contained in most retirement plans. Under this type of scheme, it's not too hard to see why the rich keep getting richer.

Despite what the traditional administrators of retirement plans want you to know, and unbeknownst to most people except the very wealthy (and their tax attorneys), the U.S. Internal Revenue Code is quite flexible with taxpayers in terms of what types of assets can be owned by a retirement plan. The simple truth is that you can own just about *any type of asset* in your retirement plan. In fact, the only types of assets you cannot own in a retirement plan are life insurance and collectibles. Collectibles includes works of art, rugs, antiques, metals, gems, jewelry, stamps, coins, alcoholic beverages, and certain other tangible personal property. There are many exceptions to this "no collectibles" rule, with the most popular exception being that your retirement plan can own gold or silver coins minted by U.S. federal or state governments.

Many people are surprised to learn that a retirement plan such as an IRA or 401(k) has the flexibility to own other assets besides stocks, bonds, and mutual funds. If you're one of these people, don't feel bad, you're certainly not alone. Currently, more than 90 percent of all retirement plans are comprised solely of these types of assets. This fact makes sense when we consider the fact that, traditionally, the people who are educating the general public about retirement plans, as I mentioned earlier, are the same people who want you to purchase assets from them to place into your retirement plan. Not only do they want you to think you *have* to purchase assets from them to place into your retirement plan, they want you to think that they *have to manage* those assets as well.

## Breaking Out of the Retirement Plan Trap

Have you ever heard the phrase "the pen is mightier than the sword?" Just as information can be powerful, the lack of information can be just as powerful because it can keep you trapped from making decisions for yourself. Let me share with you a little story I learned in law school: False imprisonment is an intentional tort, like battery or trespassing, that allows the victim to bring a civil action to recover his or her damages. Suppose the wrongdoer places the victim in a room and tells him or her that the door exiting the room is locked and that they cannot leave. As long as the victim reasonably believes that he is trapped, it doesn't matter if the door is actually unlocked. My point in telling you this is to demonstrate how the lack of information can be a trap, which is how brokerage firms have made millions of dollars by letting people think that their retirement plan options were limited.

So instead of putting the brokerage firm's assets into your retirement plan, think about the wealth you could build by putting assets of your choosing, such as real estate, options on real estate, or notes on real estate, into your retirement plan. Imagine not paying a dime in taxes on contributions to a retirement plan that is being used to purchase real estate. Even better, imagine your retirement plan owning real estate and paying zero taxes on the profits realized when that property is sold. Can you see the phenomenal growth that could be realized in your retirement dollars? The key is to tap into the vast power of this secret of the wealthy.

## THE BEST KEPT SECRET OF THE WEALTHY REVEALED

Now that you are armed with the knowledge that your retirement plan is more flexible than you may have been told, you can take advantage of this amazing opportunity. Yet, to do so, you'll still have to be willing to overcome a few hurdles.

### Understanding the Rules and Regulations Governing IRAs

You may have heard someone say that some tasks are easy, but they're not necessarily simple. An example of this might be building a model airplane: The effort required to glue the pieces together is extremely easy, yet the directions for which pieces should be glued together can be extremely complex. Having a self-directed retirement plan is similar. Generally speaking, opening up the plan, making contributions, and purchasing assets is pretty easy. However, thanks to the IRS, properly directing your retirement plan can be tricky, especially if you don't know what you're doing.

If you are analyzing a real estate transaction and you have the flexibility to purchase the assets either with funds (borrowed or cash) in your name or funds in your IRA or 401(k), you must be careful to calculate the tax advantage of your retirement plan owning the property. Any time real estate is owned by your IRA or 401(k) and you have a loan on the property, you must be careful to run an analysis that takes into account unrelated business taxable income (UBTI) issues. These are intended to prevent retirement plans from investing in income-producing businesses via direct ownership or via ownership of a partnership or LLC interest. An example might include using an IRA to buy an interest in a lumber harvesting partnership.

Let's think back to the tax benefits of retirement plans we discussed earlier: If your IRA or 401(k) invests in stocks or bonds, all dividends, interest, and gains are exempt from taxation until the funds are drawn out of a traditional IRA. If you are fortunate enough to have a Roth IRA, *all* growth, whether by dividends, interest, or capital gains is exempt from taxation. This tax-free or tax-deferred advantage of retirement plans may not always apply to real estate unless you follow the rules. If you acquire real estate without the need to borrow funds, the analysis is the same as securities, that is, using cash in your retirement plan to purchase real estate is treated the same as if you used the cash to purchase stocks, bonds, or mutual funds.

Yet, instead of using the cash in your retirement account to purchase assets on a dollar-for-dollar basis, one of the incredible advantages of using your retirement account to purchase real estate is the ability to use debt financing to leverage your liquid funds. This leverage often allows you to acquire property worth 5, 10, or even 20 times the value of your retirement plan. In other words, instead of using $20,000 in cash to purchase $20,000 in stocks, you could use the cash in your retirement plan as leverage to purchase $400,000 in real estate.

As powerful as this seems, when you borrow funds in an IRA to acquire real estate, you subject the investment to a special tax—the UBIT. The UBIT was originally enacted to require charities or tax-exempt organizations that competed with businesses that had to pay taxes to compete on a level playing field. (this change would have changed the meaning, most charities do not compete with business) However, UBIT also applies to real estate acquired by IRAs or 401(k)s with debt financing. An example of how the tax works is probably the easiest way to demonstrate its impact:

*Example 1:* Tom Taxpayer has an IRA with $100,000 and purchases a rental property for $100,000. Assuming no debt is incurred, all income and gain is exempt from UBIT. If, instead, Tom's IRA (with $100,000 of assets) purchases a $200,000 debt, using third-party debt financing to cover the other $100,000, he becomes partially subject to UBIT.

In Year 1, assume that the project returns $10,000 of cash, but after allowances for depreciation, it is only subject to income taxes on $5,000 after expenses. First, UBIT is only applicable for income tax above $1,000. Second, remember that the tax is only applied proportionately to the debt-financed portion of the project. The UBIT would equal $5,000 (taxable gain)—$1,000 (exempt amount) × 50 percent (debt financed portion) × 35 percent (in this example, the assumed trust tax rate for the year in question). The trust would pay $700 in UBIT on its gain.

*Example 2:* Same facts as Example 1, except that instead of annual rental income, the project produces no income, but appreciates over time until it is sold for $500,000 in five years. Assume that the debt has been amortized down to $50,000. The debt portion of the project is now 10 percent of the value ($50,000/$500,000).

The bottom line is that UBIT is a tax that must be considered when determining whether to use debt financing for real estate owned by an IRA. It is not, by itself, a reason not to use an IRA for real estate. Instead, it simply represents one factor that must be considered.

## Overcoming the Prohibited Transaction Rules

Because the tax impact of debt-financed projects can impact whether the project should be initiated within or without an IRA, it is important to analyze all the calculations before proceeding. While UBIT ultimately presents either a calculation issue or a minor nuisance to the use of IRAs in investing, the second hurdle to investing in real estate is what are referred to as the *prohibited transaction* rules. Violations of the prohibited transaction rules result in severe and ultimately very expensive penalty provisions that will almost without exception result in failure for an investment project. For this reason, any real estate investment needs to begin with a close analysis of the prohibited transaction rules with an eye to erring on the side of conservatism.

Failing to heed the prohibited transaction rules can result in substantial penalties and excise taxes like 100 percent of the real estate project. Violating the prohibited transaction rules can also result in immediate disqualification of your IRA.

But what are these prohibited transactions? According to the relevant statutes of the Internal Revenue Code, the following are all prohibited transactions:

a. The sale or exchange, or leasing, of any property between a plan and a disqualified person;

b. Lending of money or other extension of credit between a plan and a disqualified person;

c. Furnishing of goods, services, or facilities between a plan and a disqualified person;

d. Transfer to, or use by or for the benefit of, a disqualified person of the income or assets of a plan;

e. Act by a disqualified person who is fiduciary whereby he deals with the income or assets of a plan in his own interests or for his own account; or

f. Receipt of any consideration for his own personal account by any disqualified person who is a fiduciary from any party dealing with the plan in connection with a transaction involving the income or assets of the plan.

Considering the constant reference to "disqualified persons" in each of the prohibited transactions listed, it begs the question: What constitutes a disqualified person? A *disqualified person* would include all of the following:

- A fiduciary of the plan (this includes yourself and any advisors, such as the custodian or third-party administrator)
- Your spouse
- Lineal ascendants and descendants and their spouses (i.e., grandparents, parents, and children)
- An employer of any of the participants in a plan
- A person providing services to the plan
- Corporations, partnerships, trusts, or estates in which you own at least 50 percent of the total voting stock, either directly or indirectly

In addition, there are a few more things you must know about the operation of the prohibited transaction rules: First, you can't personally use your retirement plan-owned real estate. This simple rule should be the basis of the first question you should ask before initiating a real estate transaction with your retirement plan, that is: Do I intend to use this property personally before it is distributed to me from my IRA (and taxes are paid) or before it is sold? If the answer is yes, as is often the case for beginner investors of retirement funds, the project is not suitable for a retirement plan.

Personal use includes living in the property, even if only occasionally. I've had clients who have acquired rental properties in vacation destinations but were disappointed to discover that their use of the property, or the use by a disqualified person, is a prohibited transaction, even for properties that are available for rental income. So, if you desire to purchase a vacation property, your retirement plan is not the way to go.

For example, Sally finds a two-bedroom condominium in Deer Valley at a distressed price and acquires it for $500,000. The property is available for rent. Ultimately, the condominium rents out about 40 weeks a year. Even though the condominium would otherwise be empty for 12 weeks a year, Sally or family members are unable to use the property during those weeks because this would constitute a prohibited transaction.

Another transaction by your retirement plan that is prohibited is that your retirement plan cannot lend money to a disqualified person. This includes direct loans to children, relatives, and siblings, but would likely also include loans to businesses or entities substantially owned or controlled by disqualified persons.

One last example of a prohibited transaction is that you cannot allow a disqualified person, such as a family member, to live in property owned by your retirement plan rent free. So, if you want to provide a place for your brother-in-law to live, while at the same time building wealth for your retirement, you will not be able to do this and enjoy the tax benefits of a retirement plan.

To sum up our discussion on prohibited transactions, a violation of the prohibited transaction rules for retirement plans results in either expensive punitive excise taxes or worse, the complete disqualification of an IRA, and therefore immediate taxation. Because of the uncertainty, in the event you plan to enter into a transaction that may run afoul of the prohibited transaction rules or feel your transaction is minor or immaterial to your transaction, you have the option to seek a waiver from the Department of Labor. The Department of Labor, *not* the IRS, controls the prohibited transaction rules. In fact, you may want to contact them to see if a waiver has been granted for someone else in a similar situation. Many, many waivers have been granted to other individuals, so yours could just as easily be one of them, or may already have been allowed.

## Self-Direct Your IRA to Invest in Real Estate or Other Nontraditional Investments

You didn't think that one of those brokerage firms would help you in using funds in your retirement plan to purchase assets other than those sold by them, did you? To take control of your investment options, you have to take personal responsibility for your IRA and self-direct your investments. There are a number of trust companies that will allow you to self-direct and take control of your IRA investments.

Finding the right trust company often involves talking to other investors in your area. There are also a few firms that service clients nationwide in the real estate field.

These firms will assist with the paperwork and management of your retirement account, but will look to you to control what investments your retirement account makes. (For more information on selecting the right trust company, contact Trump University.)

Before deciding whether to self-direct your investments, you have to make an honest assessment of your investment ability. Are you currently making investment decisions or successfully buying or selling real estate? Are you making your own investment decisions for your stock and bond accounts? In either event, adding additional funds may be perfectly suited for improving or supercharging your investment results. If you find yourself overly conservative in your investment style and too scared or timid to make decisions, you may be better served using an experienced, paid investment advisor. Do not be afraid to learn and practice taking control of your investment decisions— after all, it's *your* money. Remember that your retirement account is often the sole source for income at retirement. If so, you should be cautious before using extreme leverage that may endanger your entire retirement portfolio. Trump University offers programs on learning the ins-and-outs of self-directed retirement plans as part of their course offerings. For more information, visit www.trumpuniversity.com.

As with all investments, the concept of leverage provides a tremendously powerful multiplier effect whereby you can quickly and dramatically expand your gains or losses. For example, you have an IRA worth $100,000 and use it in a 5:1 borrowing ratio to purchase real estate worth $500,000. If the property increases only 20 percent ($100,000) your return is 100 percent, thereby doubling your money. However, if your property loses 20 percent of its value, you have lost 100 percent of your initial account. A retirement account is a great place for investments that will grow in value, but potentially a very expensive place for losses or speculative investments. For this reason, it's imperative that you take the time to learn as much as possible about your investments.

## PARTNERING UP WITH OTHER PEOPLE'S MONEY

Real estate provides a means of leveraging your investments by a multiple of 10 or 20. Likewise, it provides the same opportunities for your friends, family members, and business partners. Armed with that knowledge, you have a potential source of funding for your investment ideas on a much greater scale than you might have otherwise imagined. By adding additional investors to a project, you can reduce everyone's risk and provide a greater resource pool for investment projects. This is a great way to tap into the incredible power of other people's money (OPM).

Having partners or co-investors is not for everyone. First, you will need advice or counsel to determine if securities laws will apply to a transaction involving multiple parties. Second, your group will have to have the same goals and time frames for a project to work. You do not want to be two months into a five-year project when one of your investors tells you he needs his money back. Consider the following example:

> Harry, Susan, David, Mandy, and Mike each have IRAs with $50,000 and a common goal of searching for investment properties using a debt ratio of 10 to 1. Each has the ability to borrow up to $450,000 (90 percent of a $500,000 project). If each investor borrows and invests in separate projects and three succeed (100 percent gain on the initial funds or $50,000 gain each), one posts a spectacular gain (100 percent on the entire $500,000 project or $500,000) and one fails (100 percent loss or $50,000 loss), then three will be happy, one will be ecstatic, and one investor will be extremely disappointed. If, instead, the five purchases are made through one common investment entity, then all five will achieve a gain of $120,000 on their initial $50,000 investment, and everyone's risk is lessened. Even after paying the UBIT tax, everyone's retirement account will almost double. This is the type of investment scenario they were all looking for. It's the type of arrangement that has made people wealthy for years. It can work for you if you'll simply take the time to learn how to do it.

Bottom line, buying real estate in a retirement account has many benefits over traditional investments, including the ability to use leverage, the ability to borrow funds or co-invest with funds from friends and family members, and additional creditor protection. Along with those benefits come a few hurdles like the UBIT and the prohibited transactions rules. Before proceeding, you should consult a tax advisor to assess the potential tax difference between purchasing real estate in a retirement account and purchasing real estate outside of a retirement account. Additionally, contact Trump University to find out about attending one of their in-depth training sessions on wealth preservation.

The use of self-directed strategies is a powerful way to get you miles ahead on your journey to a wealthy retirement. No wonder the wealthy keep this strategy to themselves, this really is the goose that lays the golden *nest egg*. By utilizing this astonishing tactic as part of your overall wealth-building plan, you can more rapidly propel yourself into the realm of the super wealthy. Few tools or techniques can boast the amazing combination of asset protection, tax reduction, *and* wealth accumulation benefits that a true self-directed retirement plan can give you. It's up to you to take advantage of it.

# IV

---

APPLYING THE SECRETS OF
THE WEALTHY

# 14

---

# THE MOGUL MINDSET
## STRATEGY

### APPLYING THE MULTIPRENEURING
### SECRETS OF THE WEALTHY

Through my practice of law in the fields of asset protection, tax reduction, and estate planning, one of the most common characteristics that I've observed among my wealthier clients is that they rarely pour all of their entrepreneurial energy into just one type of business. While I've worked with clients from nearly every profession, trade, or business, one thing that I've found nearly universal in my most successful clients is that they are also actively involved in the business of investing. They realize that in order to continually build up their wealth they must seek out new opportunities for growth and diversify their assets in high-yielding business endeavors.

Why this particular multibusiness phenomenon? Throughout the course of this book I've commented many times on my love of capitalism, and one of the benefits of a free-market is that, barring severe economic collapses, such as the Great Depression, if one market is down there are always other markets that are thriving. For example, if the stock market is down, the real estate market might be up. Or if the housing market is down, the stock market might be up. In short, the wealthy know not just how the economy is doing but also how particular markets are performing and they shift their entrepreneurial efforts accordingly.

Yet another reason why most of my most successful clients are involved in more than one business is because no one business operates in a vacuum. In other words, every business is, at times, both a producer *and* a consumer. Think about all of the goods and services every business must obtain in order to produce what their own customers are looking to purchase. A smart businessperson will recognize the needs of his or her company and then try to provide for those needs by creating new companies instead of turning to third parties. For example, let's consider the automotive industry. Car companies don't just produce cars out of thin air. Many car companies own assembly plants, steel and aluminum mills, advertising agencies, parts manufacturers, research and development companies, and trucking firms. Some car companies even own banks that provide financing for its customers. This strategy of becoming more of a producer and less of a consumer applies to small businesses as well. For example, an eye doctor may own his medical clinic and a glasses store. Another example would be a printing company owner who also owns an office supply store.

In sum, the most successful of my clients seem to always be looking for new markets in which to expand in order to create new wealth. I call this phenomenon the *Mogul Mindset Strategy*. Can't think of a mogul? Just look at the front cover of this book and you'll see perhaps the most famous mogul in the world, Donald Trump. As you probably know, Mr. Trump got his start in real estate but his empire now includes a television program, a clothing line, an entertainment company, hotels, casinos, product licensing, an educational company, and many more endeavors. This strategy of actively engaging in a multitude of business activities is what is sometimes referred to as *multipreneuring*. Through this activity, many wealthy business operators are able to build exponential wealth by providing services not only to their own companies but also to others.

Yet having the Mogul Mindset Strategy isn't just about opening up as many companies as you can. Instead, this strategy also involves how to effectively structure your many businesses in order to shield them from each other as well as from any liability that may attach to you personally. In this chapter, we're going to take the tools we've learned throughout this book and apply them to scenarios involving multiple businesses. In doing so, we're going to look at the two most common types of business investments in which my wealthier clients are involved: the stock market and real estate.

## STOCK MARKET WEALTH STRUCTURING

One of the first things that I counsel my clients about with regard to their stock market activities is to make sure that they structure themselves properly. Properly structuring your stock market activities isn't necessarily difficult, but it does take a bit of careful planning to be done correctly. It first begins with deciding if you want to be an investor or a trader. What's the difference? An investor is a market participant who purchases stocks for the long term with the belief that those stocks will increase in value at some point in the future. Investors are typically concerned with a stock's value and the company's success over a long duration of time. These are the types of market participants who purchase stocks as a way to save for retirement or for their children's college education. Typically an investor is an individual, but investment banks and mutual funds fall into the category of investors as well. In sum, an investor looks to accumulate wealth over a long period of time.

By contrast, a trader is a person, qualified by the IRS, who is primarily in the business of buying and selling stocks to the point where trading is treated as "a trade or business." Stated another way, a trader can be defined as a person who buys and sells securities for his or her personal account, not on behalf of clients. A person who trades with someone else's money would have a harder time making a case for trader status because the time he or she devotes to trading his or her own account would be limited.

But why does this differentiation between an investor and a trader matter? For most people, achieving trader status is preferred because as a trader in securities, your gain or loss from the disposition of securities is not taken into account when you figure net earnings from self-employment. For investors, deductions are limited to $3000 per year and any expenses associated with the investing activity can only be claimed as miscellaneous itemized deductions—and those have to exceed 2 percent of their adjusted gross income (AGI) to get any deduction at all. One exception to this is investment interest expense, which can be deducted as a normal interest deduction on Schedule A to the extent of earned interest and dividend income. For traders, on the other hand, deductions are much more plentiful. For this reason, trader status is highly advantageous.

A trader reports his expenses (as an individual) on Schedule C. This means that the expenses are 100 percent deductible—without regard to the AGI limitations one encounters on Schedule A. And if the trader elects mark-to-market accounting for his stock trading, the losses incurred in any particular year are not limited to $3000. And he does not need to worry about wash sales. Typical deductions for traders include:

- Subscriptions to newsletters
- The monthly fee for Internet access (presuming you trade via the Internet)
- Cable fees for CNBC (if you utilize this for financial and trading news)
- Brokerage account management fees
- Interest on loans used to fund your trading business
- Books and seminars related to your trading business
- Travel expenses associated with attending trading seminars
- Data retrieval services

- Trading advice
- Computers and other equipment used in your trading business (they may need to be depreciated)
- Legal fees
- Bookkeeping, accounting, and tax preparation fees
- Other trading related expenses

Now that we've looked a little bit at taxes, let's focus on asset protection strategies for stock market participants. As you've already learned in this book, at the heart of any asset protection strategy are business entities. As we also already know, corporations and limited liability companies give their owners, shareholders, officers, and members, asset protection benefits. This means that although traders run the risk of losing their initial investments in their trading business, they will not be personally liable for the creditors of the business, such as margin calls. Limited partnerships, on the other hand, only give asset protection benefits to the limited partners. But for reasons we will discuss in a moment, they can be crucial to your trading business and there are structures that can be created to eliminate the general partner's liability issue.

Regardless of which entity you utilize for trading, in order to achieve this asset protection benefit, the entity must be structured properly. First and foremost, the brokerage account or accounts must be in the name of the entity. This is imperative. Second, all trading activities should be done in the name of the entity rather than in your individual name. Third, the entity should have its own bank account so that the entity's and the trader's assets are not commingled. If such commingling exists, a court or the IRS can find that the entity is merely an "alter-ego" of the individual, which means that you would lose the corporate veil of protection. This goes along with my final word of advice, which is that all formalities associated with the entity should be strictly adhered to. The entity should have its own employer identification number (EIN) and its corporate records such as minutes of meetings should be adequately maintained. If these formalities are not followed, it is further evidence that the trader's business entity is not separate and distinct from the trader individually, and again the corporate veil can be pierced.

Probably the most beneficial entity type for stock market participants is the limited partnership. As we mentioned previously, a limited partnership has two types of partners: limited partners, who are investors and have no management authority over partnership affairs and have limited liability; and general partners, who control the activities of the partnership and have *un*limited liability.

This entity doesn't sound exactly favorable, until we learn how to structure a limited partnership with a corporation for the maximum benefits to you. Here's how it works. The brokerage account is held inside the limited partnership. The limited partnership is managed by its general partner, in this case, a corporation. The individual trader, and potentially his family members, would be the limited partners. The corporation, with built-in limited liability, has now eliminated the general partner asset protection conundrum. Now the corporation with limited liability, not the trader individually, would be personally liable for any debts or obligations of the trader's business that cannot be satisfied by the business' assets.

Turning once again to the issue of taxes, this limited partnership corporation structure does have significant tax benefits. The corporation would pay for expenses of trading and seek reimbursement from the limited partnership. The corporation could also charge a management fee to the limited partnership to split monies between the individuals and the corporation. The corporation would also be entitled to a small percentage (usually 1 percent) of the profits earned in the limited partnership. The end result is that you are generating a tremendous amount of legitimate business deductions by virtue of using the corporation as the management company. In the end, you have a great deal of control over what income actually flows onto your individual tax return. The monies you receive as a limited partner remain unearned and not subject to self-employment tax and can be either long term or short term.

## REAL ESTATE WEALTH STRUCTURING

As already noted, perhaps the most common business that my most affluent clients pursue is real estate. For centuries, the wealth of individuals has been measured by how much property they own. Even today, while the market might ebb and flow, real estate continues to appreciate over the long term creating enormous amounts of wealth. One of the secrets of real estate investing that the wealthy know and use to their advantage is the system of leveraging. Whenever someone purchases real estate, they typically use little (if any) of their own money to purchase their property. How do they purchase these properties without having their own money invested to pay for it? The answer is that they utilize other people's money (OPM). The bulk of the money used to purchase real estate comes from other people, such as a bank or other lender. Yet even though one may only pay a fraction (if any) of the property's purchase price, that investor still owns 100 percent of the rights in the property. Better yet, when the property appreciates and is sold, that investor keeps 100 percent of the profits.

So how do the wealthy structure their real estate holdings? The key is to operate each property, or group of properties, as separate businesses. To do this, the first step is to establish business entities to hold title to your real estate. For my clients who invest in real estate or are looking into getting into the market, I typically recommend that they start with a limited liability company or limited partnership. Why is this? As we've learned already, limited liability companies (LLCs) and limited partnerships (LPs) offer asset protection for their members and partners, respectfully, so that the debts and liabilities of the entity are not the responsibility of its owners. Of course, in a limited partnership the general partner would be personally responsible for the debts and liabilities of the partnership, but we've already discussed strategies for overcoming this pitfall through the use of a corporation as the general partner.

As you might expect, asset protection is critical for the entrepreneur who is in the real estate business. The types of possible lawsuits that the real estate investor can face are virtually limitless, but can include:

- Creditor lawsuits
- Slip and fall cases
- Catastrophic injury
- Construction defects
- Environmental issues
- Government fines/taxes

Aside from the asset protection benefits, LLCs and LPs are perfect for real estate investors because of their tax benefits. First, these entities can help you save on capital gains taxes. LLCs and LPs are pass-through entities, which, as you will recall, means that they are taxed only at the individual level. Capital gains tax rates are lower for individuals than for corporations since corporations have their own tax obligation that must be met before the potential double taxation that could result once the income is passed on to its owners. What this means is that if you realize a capital gain on a property held in an LLC or LP, you will save money on taxes. More money means the ability to invest in more properties.

The pass-through taxation of LLCs and LPs can also be a tax benefit, especially in the early years of your real estate businesses, because any losses sustained by the business would be a deduction on your personal income tax return. When you start a new business, especially if you've invested a large amount of money into a property that you intend to hold for more than a year, your business is initially going to show a loss. A particularly powerful use of this tax benefit is to stagger your new real estate businesses so that you can receive a large tax deduction every year to help offset your capital gains achieved by your then-existing entities.

The most powerful tax benefit of LLCs and LPs that is particularly useful for real estate businesses stems from the fact that these two business entities have *free transferability of assets*. This means that money or other assets can be moved into or out of the business without such contribution or distribution being a taxable event. For example, suppose you wish to purchase a property in an LLC and a large down payment is required. Thanks to the benefit of free transferability of assets you can deposit the requisite funds into the LLC's account without any tax consequences. Additionally, when the LLC sells the property, it can then pay you back that same amount of money, again without any tax consequences.

As you learned in Part II of this book, insurance is another tool that can be used for asset protection purposes. For real estate investors, insurance is of course very popular, and often times required. Yet, it deserves mention that insurance is not a substitute for comprehensive asset protection planning. Again, every insurance policy has two shortcomings: insurance policies will only cover certain types of events, and every insurance policy has its limit. Remember, never put all of your eggs in one basket, even if that basket is insured.

After establishing an entity, or entities depending on the number of properties you own, the next step is to operate your real estate business *as* a business. Foremost, you must keep separate books and bank accounts for each of your entities. We've already discussed the activities that can lead to a loss of asset protection benefits, known as piercing the corporate veil, and by commingling the paperwork and funds of your entities you may protect your personal assets, but your businesses may lose the asset protection from each other.

Another step in effectively setting up your business entities is to make proper use of deductions. To do this, you have to establish proper bookkeeping methods, as we discussed. Pursuant to Internal Revenue Code Section 162(a), a business can deduct all "ordinary and necessary expenses" incurred in carrying on a trade or business. The following deductions are available for your real estate business:

- Business equipment such as computers
- Utilities for your office

- Auto allowances
- Home office expenses
- Educational expenses such as real estate conferences or seminars
- Business furniture such as chairs or desks
- Medical expenses through the use of a medical reimbursement plan
- Many other "ordinary and necessary" expenses

## CONCLUSION

Do you have the Mogul Mindset Strategy? Remember, being a mogul is not about setting up as many different companies as possible. Rather, being a mogul is about diversifying your time, effort, and energy into multiple business endeavors that can produce multiple sources of income. It also involves properly structuring all of your various business endeavors so that they can all receive the maximum asset protection and tax reduction benefits as possible. Review your current types of businesses to determine how you can apply the Mogul Mindset Strategy to your own situation, and reap the same success as the moguls who have preceded you.

# 15

---

# ASSET PROTECTION IN
# ACTION

## *How the Rich Put It All Together*

I have found that as an attorney, a teacher to my thousands of seminar students, and as a student of all of my diverse areas of study, I can read about the various methods and strategies of any given area, whatever the topic, and gain a certain base level of understanding. As helpful as that may be, the best way to truly understand complex concepts and strategies is to look at real-world examples of those concepts and strategies in use.

Now that you have learned the secrets of growing and protecting wealth, let's take a look at some actual case studies that illustrate these principles *in action*. The clients have been disguised to protect their privacy, but the facts are actual cases. As you read these case studies, keep in mind the blending principles you learned in Chapters 5 and 9. Also, try to think of alternate ways to accomplish estate planning, tax reduction, and asset protection goals. From working with my clients over the years, I've come to realize that when many strategies will lead to the same result, the *best strategy* may be the one that the client feels most comfortable using.

## Case Study 1

About two years ago, Melinda called me for advice on protecting her assets. Her situation was especially urgent because she had considerable unprotected assets and her family had a high-risk, successful plumbing business that she ran with her husband as a general partnership.

Melinda keeps the books and makes appointments for the plumbing business while her husband Bill, their two adult sons, and two part-time, contracted employees do the field work. Between the rapid growth of the business and the frequent storm and erosion damage in the area, the business grosses around $600,000 a year and nets a comfortable $180,000 to $200,000 in profit.

Melinda and her family live in a rapidly developing area on 40 acres that Melinda inherited. They own the entire property with no liens or mortgages, and 30 years ago they built their home on 10 acres of that property (tract A). The home is owned without debt as well. Bill and Melinda had the property surveyed and divided into four 10-acre tracts so that their two sons could build on two of the three remaining tracts (tracts B and C) in the future if they wished. The fourth tract (tract D) was originally used for the storefront of the business and business equipment, but they have since moved this into a new leased storefront with higher traffic in town, this fourth tract is unused as well. With the growth in the area of their home, their three undeveloped 10-acre tracks are worth about $150,000 to $200,000 each and the fourth tract, along with their home, is worth a combined $480,000.

In their mid-fifties, Melinda and Bill were both a little concerned that they put too much of their income and savings back into the business each year, instead of putting enough away for retirement. Bill dreams of passing the business to his sons and retiring in a few years, but their retirement savings won't allow it.

In addition to these assets, they have other savings and investments of around $40,000 in various modest return investment funds.

In summary, their assets are as follows:

*Tract A:* 10 acres and their home worth $480,000

*Tracts B and C:* 10 undeveloped acres worth about $150,000 to $200,000 each held for their sons' future use

*Tract D:* 10 undeveloped acres worth about $150,000 to $200,000

*Plumbing business:* Grosses about $600,000 a year and nets $180,000 in profit.

*Inventory and equipment:* $150,000

*Investments:* $40,000

Melinda attended one of our seminars and knows that she and Bill are completely vulnerable and she wants to establish a wealth structure as quickly as possible. Because their assets are unprotected, you can see how thrilled an attorney might be to file a lawsuit against them.

Based on what you've learned so far, do you have any ideas as to how their assets can be protected?

First, the general partnership structure for the plumbing business is the biggest risk to their assets, so they definitely need to place the business into some sort of limited liability business entity. In this instance, I would suggest an S corporation that will give Melinda and Bill complete protection from the debts and liabilities of the business, while at the same time allowing them to set up certain fringe benefits, such as a medical reimbursement plan and a traditional IRA.

But what about all of the business equipment? These assets can be protected by putting them into a holding entity that is separate from the plumbing business. With this structure, the corporation containing the plumbing business would be conducting all business activities and thus incurring all the risk. In other words, the plumbing service does the work and *owns* nothing. The plumbing business would then lease the equipment from the holding entity. Therefore, the holding entity would own the equipment, but does no activities with it.

In addition, Bill and Melinda can establish a blend of retirement plans, some traditional through the two corporations, and some true self-directed plans, to save the maximum in retirement funds so that they can meet their retirement goals.

Properties B, C, and D should go into three separate limited partnerships or LLCs, since two tracts may be transferred to their sons at some time in the future. The fourth parcel of land (tract D) could be sold or leased in the future, so a separate entity for that is essential.

Tract A, along with their home, should be put into a living trust. This living trust should also hold their ownership interests in the various business entities. Remember, these steps aren't made for asset protection purposes because a living trust offers no such benefits. Rather, this recommendation is made for estate planning purposes.

To make this even clearer, look at Figure 15.1 for how all of this works.

That seems like a lot of entities, a lot of trouble, and a lot of expense. But let's face it, one accident, one bad business deal, or one frivolous lawsuit could wipe them out *completely*. They have over a million dollars

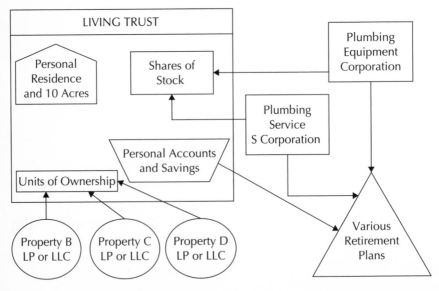

**Figure 15.1   Melinda and Bill's Strategy**

in assets out there for anyone to take. With no protection, they are "easy pickings!"

In addition, there are other benefits to creating this structure that, in the future will more than pay for the cost of establishing that structure:

- By splitting the plumbing business, they are moving part of the business into another entity, the C corporation, which is taxed in its own bracket and can potentially save them thousands each year in taxes.
- They will also gain the benefit of beefed up retirement plans so that they can retire in comfort. With properly structured retirement planning, they will also experience tax savings through tax-deferred (or tax-free) growth, as well as asset protection for much or all of their retirement money.
- They have reduced or eliminated the cost of probate and potentially reduced or eliminated inheritance taxes for their children through proper estate planning with their living trust. Their children will also receive the benefit of a stepped up basis in the inherited property with the living trust.
- Because the vacant tracts of land and the commercial assets are now placed into entities, they can more easily convey those assets to their sons by transferring the stock in the plumbing business through gifting.

## CASE STUDY 2

This next case study is a good example of using fringe benefits to save taxes for your business as well as providing tax-free benefits for yourself and your employees.

Howard was referred to us for help with his tax and business planning. Howard ran a profitable computer repair business that employed him and two employees. The computer repair store was operated as a sole proprietorship. Howard was concerned about his tax bill from the previous year and came to us for help. In discussing Howard's business, we learned that Howard did not have any health insurance nor did he provide any health insurance for his employees. This was particularly disconcerting to Howard because every time he would properly train an employee they would be hired away by a larger company offering benefits, causing Howard the time and expense to hire and train a replacement.

What can Howard do to maximize his business deductions while at the same time offer incentives for his employees to remain loyal to his business?

First and foremost, Howard needs to place his business into some sort of limited liability business entity that provides him with asset protection benefits. As you have learned, by operating as a sole proprietorship, Howard was *personally liable* for any debts or liabilities of his computer repair business. For reasons that I will explain in a moment, we recommended that Howard incorporate his business rather than placing it into another type of business entity.

Turning now to lowering the business' tax bill (which until now had been passed through to Howard every year since the business was a sole proprietorship), Howard and I agreed that one of the best ways to offset some of the business' profits was to offer appropriate fringe benefits to Howard and his other employees. When it comes to providing fringe benefits, the best entity to accomplish this is the C corporation.

The first fringe benefit Howard set up through the corporation was a health insurance benefit. Medical insurance premiums paid for owners and employees of a corporation are entirely tax deductible. Because we selected a C corporation, Howard's business also elected to establish a medical reimbursement plan that could cover medical expenses not covered by insurance. Any money spent pursuant to the medical reimbursement plan was also entirely tax deductible.

Next, Howard set up a retirement benefits package for himself and his employees. Dollar for dollar, retirement benefits are the most valuable tax-deductible fringe benefit a corporation can offer.

Another popular fringe benefit that corporations offer to certain employees is a company vehicle, and Howard wanted to take advantage of this deduction as well. Vehicles can be a business deduction in a couple of different ways. First, an officer can keep up with the business mileage of the vehicle and reimburse himself or herself at a rate per mile designated by the Internal Revenue Service (currently $0.445 per mile). With this method, Howard would not be able to deduct actual expenses of the vehicle, but the amount he would be paying from the business to himself would be a business deduction and tax-free income to Howard personally. The second way to obtain a deduction from a company vehicle is by using the actual expenses of the vehicle and depreciating the cost of the vehicle in an entity. This would allow Howard to deduct those expenses that are usually more in the first couple of years and then, after the vehicle is paid for and the depreciation runs out, the deduction continues to decrease.

The final fringe benefit Howard elected to provide to himself and his employees was educational benefits. Like vehicle fringe benefits, educational benefits can be deducted in two ways. First, educational expenses that are directly related to your job are entirely tax deductible so long as the expense is reasonable. For example, if Howard paid for one of his employees to attend a computer course at a local vocational college, this expense would be entirely tax deductible. The second way that educational expenses can be deducted is by starting an educational assistance plan. With this type of plan, a business can deduct all educational expenses, even those that are nonbusiness related, but only up to an amount of $5,250 per year per employee.

Finally, as if Howard's new benefits policy was not enough to help him retain valuable employees, by operating his computer repair business as a corporation, he now has the luxury of rewarding his employees with corporate shares. Moreover, to ensure that Howard would always retain control of his corporation as it grew, he elected that the shares rewarded to his employees would be nonvoting shares.

## Case Study 3

Robin is a cosmetologist and massage therapist who recently began investing in real estate in hopes of supplementing her income. Robin is enjoying a comfortable lifestyle from her full-time job, but is basically a sole proprietor who leases space from the salon owner. Additionally, as a sole proprietor, she has few, if any benefits. Seeing that she needed to establish her own benefit plans and residual income, Robin began investing with a coworker who took real estate investment courses with her. Additionally, the salon owner, who didn't understand real estate investing, agreed to invest cash to help fund the deals that Robin and her coworker would find and put together.

Since they were all "pals" from work, the ladies had no formal entities or agreements other than their word for each of the deals. They basically operated on a "hand-shake agreement" whereby each received a portion of any of the cash flow from each investment, depending on how much work or cash they had put into that deal, respectively, and their ownership percentages varied accordingly.

In addition to partnership with her pals from work, Robin had taken some of her extra cash from the real estate deals and had begun "flipping" a property or two every year. The other two ladies weren't really interested in this venture, but Robin and her 12-year-old son Dean really enjoyed finding, fixing up, and selling properties.

Since they got along well and seemed to have a knack for finding properties that gave them at least a small cash flow, Robin and the other two ladies were perfectly happy with the hand-shake agreement that they had.

After being in business for a few years, Robin realized that not only was she personally liable for her investments, but for the liability of her two partners as well. She also realized that they had no buyout or right-of-first refusal agreements if one of the three ladies wanted or needed to get out of a deal. Robin was relatively frugal and quite the saver, and she realized that her wealth was threatened by her fellow investors' debt.

After Robin's realization of how much her assets were at risk, she came into my office asking how she should structure her wealth and business dealings so as to provide the best asset protection, tax reduction, and estate planning benefits possible.

Our first job was to identify the holes in Robin's business structure and suggest ways to rectify the situation. We quickly discovered that Robin, individually, and together with her two pals, had by default set up the two worst types of business structures—the sole proprietorship and general partnership. Our next job was to help Robin restructure her business and personal assets.

Before even trying to counsel Robin on asset protection issues, we first had to think about estate planning because she was also a single parent. Accordingly, we set Robin up with all the essential estate planning tools, the most important of which was a living trust. Robin's living trust would hold all of her personal assets, including her personal residence, modest investment accounts, and transfer those assets to her son outside of probate. Additionally, her living trust was drafted such that the trustee would hold and manage the trust estate for the benefit of her son until he reached the age of 25. We also included a provision in Robin's estate plan that would appoint a guardian for Dean should she pass away before his eighteenth birthday.

With Robin's estate planning out of the way, we next had to attack her asset protection woes. Each of the properties owned by Robin and her two pals in the general partnership were fairly new purchases with little or no equity. Therefore, we decided to put the four properties into two LLCs. Additionally, we executed specific operating agreements for each.

Robin elected to have her ownership interests in the two LLCs managed by a corporation that we created for her. Through this corporation, Robin could establish a retirement plan that she didn't have at the present, and could provide any other benefits she needed for the corporation's officers and employees, (i.e., her and her son) such as medical coverage.

Next, for Robin's real estate ventures with her son, since she was involved in "flipping" properties, we established a limited partnership with a corporation as the general partner. With this ownership structure, Robin and Dean were not personally liable for the debts and liabilities of the LP over and above the assets in each entity. Moreover, the income that was paid to Robin and Dean was not subject to self-employment taxes, and the cash transferred to the general partner (the corporation) was used to fund her retirement plan. Robin is pretty successful at this venture, and her stylist friend and partner is beginning to show interest. Eventually, Robin wants to establish a true, self-directed IRA and have her friend work with her to flip the properties. Robin really hopes her friend will establish a retirement plan as well as she is in her late 40s and has no retirement plan in place for her future.

With all that in mind, take a look at the, relatively simple structure we have in place for Robin, along with her two partners (Figure 15.2).

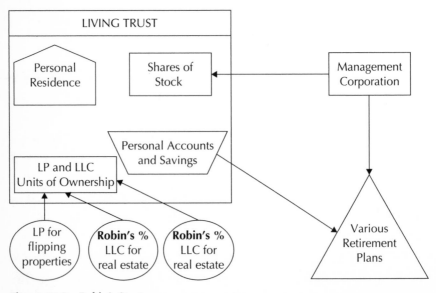

**Figure 15.2   Robin's Strategy**

## CASE STUDY 4

The next case study helps to illustrate the blending of multiple properties for asset protection purposes.

Jude, a Nevada resident, wanted to start a pet supply company in Las Vegas with $200,000 of capital. Jude expects to purchase a small building to use as a warehouse and retail store, two delivery trucks, and office equipment. Jude expects to fill his warehouse with inventory purchased on credit directly from the manufacturers. Jude asked me for advice on how best to structure his commercial investment so that it would be safe from any personal or business creditors.

To complicate matters, Jude is expected in the near future to inherit a motorcycle shop from his uncle who is dying of cancer. Jude's uncle is not a shrewd businessman and he currently runs the motorcycle shop as a sole proprietorship. Jude is concerned that he may be inheriting all of the debts of the motorcycle shop and he is concerned about these creditors reaching the assets of his new pet supply business.

How many entities, at a minimum, should Jude utilize in his asset protection strategy?

At least two. As we discussed in Chapter 9, it is always best to separate a business' assets from the arm of the business that is engaged in commerce with the public. Accordingly, we suggested to Jude that he form at least two LLCs. One LLC would serve as the operating entity and would purchase the business' inventory on credit and sell the inventory to the public. Jude's second entity would serve as the holding company that would own the warehouse/retail building as well as the delivery trucks and office equipment. This holding company would then lease these assets to the operating entity, for a fee.

Regarding setting up these two entities, we first formed the holding company. Jude then contributed the $200,000 to this entity in return for his membership interest in the LLC. We then formed a separate operating entity. Since the operating entity is going to be the one actively engaged in commerce, and thus risking exposure, having the operating entity owned solely by the holding company just adds one more layer of protection between Jude and the operating entity.

Finally, we had to address Jude's concern over his inheritance and whether any creditors of the sole proprietorship, if they subsequently became creditors of Jude, could attach his interests in his pet supply business. In most states, an inheritance or gift can be specifically disclaimed, and Jude certainly has this option. Suppose that Jude does inherit his uncle's motorcycle shop, and the debt later becomes Jude's. Would these creditors be able to attach to the pet supply company? No. In Nevada and 12 other states, state law prevents personal creditors from foreclosing on an owner's LLC interests or forcing a liquidation of the business held by the LLC to satisfy purely personal debts.

By properly structuring Jude's assets through appropriate legal entities, we were able to assist him in protecting his assets from potential legal threats.

## Final Thoughts

These case studies should help you to create your own wealth protection structure. As you work with your team to create your own structure, refer back to the parts of these very different samples to determine what might best suit your particular needs in order to reach your asset protection, estate planning, and tax reduction goals. Don't be discouraged if your situation seems vastly different from the ones listed here. There are as many variations as there are individuals. Yours will not look exactly like the ones above, but they should give you the confidence to begin implementing your own personal wealth protection strategies. The more you work with it, the more adept and confident you will become in structuring. The information contained in the final two chapters will assist you in putting together your team as well as designing a corresponding course of action.

# 16

---

## THE ASSET PROTECTION TEAM

### *Finding Counter-Attack Specialists That Handle the Dirty Work*

Achieving phenomenal success in any endeavor involves surrounding yourself with those who make you better. This is *essential* to your overall success. It is perhaps the best advice you will ever receive. Will this cost you some money? Certainly. More importantly, however, it will not cost you anywhere near as much as it would, had you not sought advice. It is an investment that will reap phenomenal returns.

Much of the work involved in setting up and administering your wealth protection plan is relatively straightforward and routine. Any knowledgeable and motivated person can effectively accomplish much of this themselves. However, you *will* need assistance from others from time to time. Some of the decisions you must make will involve complex areas of law and/or taxation and are best directed to qualified professionals. The bottom line is to seek out the assistance of those who are experienced in these areas. This chapter is designed to help you in your search.

## Your "Master Mind" Team

One of the most important steps you will ever take to preserve the wealth you have accumulated is to build your "Master Mind" team. This team consists of those professionals who can give you much-needed assistance in areas that require more specialized knowledge. This includes a variety of different professionals—specialized tools for your toolbox. You need several members on your team because of the varied situations you will face.

In building your team, here are a few suggestions of who you may need:

- Attorney
- Accountant
- Tax advisor
- Insurance agent
- Real estate agent
- Stockbroker/Financial planner
- Spouse
- Retirement specialist

While all of the team members are important to your overall success, I want to pay particular attention to the two that will be most beneficial to you in establishing and administering your wealth protection plan, your attorney and your tax advisor.

Before we talk about these important team members, do not make the mistake of thinking that you can just save the money and do it all yourself. Too many times people end up doing what I refer to as, "tripping over pennies on their way to dollars." A Master Mind team can be the quintessential ingredient to your overall success.

## Your Attorney

One of the most important members of your team will be your attorney. When it comes to pure business and legal decisions, no one member plays as large a role in the overall success of your operations as does your attorney. For this reason, it is imperative that you find an attorney who will be an asset to your team.

You do not need a high-dollar, big-firm corporate lawyer for all of your legal issues. Not to minimize the value of a good lawyer, but specialized legal services should be reserved for specialized legal work. In identifying an attorney for your team, talk with other people who may be able to provide the names of lawyers who understand the type of work you are needing and who they feel comfortable and confident with when dealing with their own financial and estate planning concerns. Speak with business associates within your own company or even friends and relatives who may have names of possible attorneys to help with your particular situation.

Should you decide to seek out a specialist for a more complicated legal matter, there are a few issues you must pay particular attention to. After you have acquired the names of a few key prospects, don't wait until a legal crisis occurs before making your initial contact. If you put the contact off until things are chaotic, you may not have sufficient time to find a lawyer who will work with you at an affordable price. In fact, it's extremely possible that you may end up settling for the first available person at a moment's notice. This almost always results in an unfavorable situation where you will pay too much for too little.

I learned this the hard way in a nonlegal area several years ago when I was building my home. I contracted the project myself and was responsible for lining up all of the subcontractors. After being strung along by one of these subs, I was left in a position where I needed the work done ASAP. I called around and found the first available person to handle the job and was rather dissatisfied with the end result. I blame myself for this unfortunate situation because I let myself get into a situation where I had almost no choice but to take the first available person. In retrospect, it is not surprising that I did not get the optimal results. If this person was available immediately, this should have told me something: He didn't have any work. Why is that? Even if you are able to get a top-notch professional to do the job, if you wait until the last minute, you will certainly pay for it.

When you do contact a lawyer, state your intentions in advance. Tell him or her that you are looking for someone who is willing to give you guidance, get you pointed in the right direction, and to tackle those important legal issues you may find yourself faced with. Let the attorney know that you intend to compensate him for his assistance. You'll want to address fees right from the start. It may be an uncomfortable subject to raise, but let me assure you that it is much less comfortable to bring it up down the road.

It is always best to get a clear understanding of how fees will be calculated. Ask the attorney specifically what it will cost for the job. Ask how you will be billed for this work. Some lawyers bill a flat amount for a call or conference, while others bill to the nearest time interval (such as 6-, 10- or 20-minute intervals). A standard practice in firms is to bill in 6-minute increments. The premise is that it takes at least six minutes to do anything once you document it in detail for billing purposes. The most important thing is to understand the billing process to avoid surprises. Additionally, it is always a good idea to get fee arrangements in writing in the form of an engagement letter. Any lawyer should understand this completely. The written document provides evidence of everyone's understanding should it be needed. The simple rule I like to follow is: *I would rather have it and not need it, than need it and not have it.*

## YOUR TAX ADVISOR

Becoming proficient in the area of taxation is a huge task. To truly master all of the tax information applicable to you is almost impossible if you're not planning on devoting yourself to it full time. The good news is that you don't have to become an expert in the field of taxation to preserve your wealth for yourself and your family. Once you're equipped with a firm base level of knowledge, it is more advisable to find a good tax advisor to become a member of your Master Mind team.

There are many different types of tax advisors to choose from. One problem, however, is that the tax field is somewhat unregulated so you need to be careful and find someone who is an expert rather than someone who merely claims to be an expert. What you're really looking for is someone who is experienced in helping people in your particular situation rather than someone who offers a one-size-fits-all plan. At the same time, there is seldom any need to seek the assistance of a certified public accountant with one of the big public accounting firms for your basic day-to-day issues.

Ideally, you need a financial professional who understands the type of situation in which you're involved. When it comes to matters of estate planning and the tax consequences related to structuring your estate, I recommend that you speak with a tax attorney. Typically, tax attorneys are your best team members when it comes to implementing various estate planning and wealth preservation strategies. However, you will also need someone who can assist you in filing various tax returns.

The following is a list of some of the professionals who may be of assistance to you, listed in the order of their specialized knowledge:

- *Tax return preparer:* You may have seen offers by large accounting companies to enroll in their "tax schools" to learn how to prepare taxes. People who have taken such courses, who refer to themselves as tax return preparers, typically do not have degrees in accounting or business, do not have any sort of state certification, and are not licensed through the Internal Revenue Service (IRS). Some states impose their own requirements but most simply allow anyone to prepare tax forms. These folks may sometimes be extremely knowledgeable about the subject of taxes or they may not be, you take your chances. Be careful.

- *Enrolled agent:* An enrolled agent is a person who is licensed by the IRS as a tax preparer and advisor. To obtain this license, the person must pass a test administered by the IRS or have at least five years of experience working for the IRS. Of the tax professionals available, enrolled agents are typically the least expensive.

- *Tax attorney:* A tax attorney will typically be the most expensive source of tax assistance, but he or she can also be the most valuable. A tax attorney has chosen to specialize in the area of taxation as it relates to individuals and, more specifically, to legal entities such as corporations, trusts, partnerships, LLCs, and retirement plans. Instead of hiring an attorney who has a general practice, these specialized professionals should be retained in the event that you find yourself with a serious tax problem, require legal representation in court, or have a legal problem with the IRS. They may also be of great assistance for complex tax and estate planning issues as well.

- *Certified public accountant (CPA):* Finally, we have our friends the CPAs. CPAs are licensed and regulated in each state and are required to pass an extensive examination prior to obtaining their license. A CPA cannot negotiate with the IRS on your behalf or represent you in court, rather, they perform sophisticated accounting duties for individuals and businesses and/or prepare complex tax forms and returns. Simply stated, a CPA can be one of your greatest allies when it comes to business tax advice. Remember that just because someone is a CPA does not mean that they have the necessary tax or business knowledge to assist you. Not all CPAs are proficient in the topic of taxes or in the specific type of business in which you are engaged. Bottom line: *You need a specialist when it comes to taxes, so make sure you find one who understands your situation, your business, your goals, and your objectives.*

One of the best ways to find a good fit for your tax advisor is to ask other people if they know someone with specific expertise. If you can get the names of a few candidates, you can take it from there and begin the interview process. The information you learned in choosing an attorney is applicable here as well. Make sure to find someone with whom you are both comfortable and confident. These Master Mind team members will be integral parts of your business as a whole, so choose those who you enjoy dealing with and who understand that they are members of a team. Far too often, professionals will try to demonstrate their purported intelligence by creating obstacles and raising objections to information you receive from other team members. While this can sometimes be valid, remember that you pay your professionals for their areas of expertise, not for their personal opinions.

The final consideration when choosing your tax team member is the fees associated with tax advice. Tax professionals may not be cheap, but their advice can pay for itself. Realize that the fees you pay for obtaining good tax assistance is part of the investment in your wealth plan. A good tax professional can save you far more than he ever charges you. With that in mind, let's take a look at tax fees.

It is always a good idea to develop a clear understanding of how any fees will be imposed as early in the relationship as possible. Specifically, you need to know if fees will be charged on an hourly or flat fee basis. The most common type of billing practice among professionals is to charge hourly. These fees can range anywhere from $50 per hour to as high as $500 per hour (and even more), depending on the type of professional you use.

Remember the advice regarding getting things in writing when establishing your relationship with your attorney. This is also the case when dealing with your tax professional. You should ask for a written agreement before any work is done so that everyone knows exactly where they stand. Once again, *it's better to have it and not need it, than to need it and not have it.*

One of the things that people love about the wealth protection seminars we conduct is that we provide information dealing with asset protection, estate and retirement planning, *and* tax reduction. Rather than having to seek out separate team members for each of these areas, we are able to provide our students and potential clients with professionals who understand their needs and who can help them to accomplish their individual goals and objectives. If you would like to attend one of these events, contact Trump University for more information.

Remember, building your Master Mind team is one of the most critical ingredients to your overall success. When dealing with an issue of this importance, it is essential that you spend a little time making the decisions as to who will become a part of this team. Top legal and tax professionals are not cheap, but they can be worth their weight in gold when used properly. Above all, make sure that you find members for your team who make your business and life better. Always remember that the money you spend on top-level assistance is not an expense, it is an investment.

# 17

A CALL TO ACTION

In many ways, I believe that this is the most important chapter in the book. Not because it contains the most crucial information on legal entities or the inner workings of your asset protection plan, but because it covers the most quintessential ingredient to your success. In fact, if you lack this portion, your success will be greatly limited if not prohibited. That essential element is *action*. Understand, I am in no way minimizing the importance of learning. Gaining knowledge is one of the most important endeavors a person could undertake. My belief in this is evidenced by the fact that I have dedicated my life to the production and dissemination of educational tools that enable people to gain valuable legal and financial knowledge. But I need to ask you a question. If you have all the information, yet fail to act on it, how much good does it do you?

Think about it. What does that tell you? Does that mean that there is no need for knowledge? Of course not! But you must balance these issues. The best way to illustrate this point is to take a look at an example that I go through in my seminars. During the seminar, I ask the attendees to raise their hands if they: (1) have children that they are putting through college right now, (2) have put their children through college in the past, or (3) put themselves through college. I have them keep their hands up through the next question which is: How many of you deducted that expense? Invariably, nearly every hand in the room goes down.

The next question is one of the most telling: Why not? Why aren't you deducting these expenses? There are certain specific restrictions on whether these expenses are deductible. Too many times, however, people fail to deduct expenses that they could have deducted.

When I ask people why they neglected to take the deduction, the answer is usually because they didn't know about it. They simply did not know that they could take this deduction. This is the first problem that comes up, *lack of knowledge*. It is very difficult to take advantage of benefits when you don't know about them. Knowledge is crucial, but you need to be careful about the knowledge you are receiving and believing. Let me give you an example.

As I mentioned, after I ask the question about deducting educational expenses, my next question is: Why not? The response I get is important because it demonstrates the type of information being disseminated. I have many people who tell me that they didn't deduct this expense because their accountant told them that they couldn't take that deduction.

Let me begin by saying that the accountant is right. *They* can't take that deduction. The problem is that they didn't ask their accountant the right question. The accountant answered the question that was asked. As such, they got the answer to *that* question. Do you sometimes feel like you're getting the wrong answers out of life? Perhaps the difficulty is that you're asking the wrong questions. Asking the right questions falls under the category of knowledge. You need to know the right questions to ask if you are looking for the answers that you want. I want to show you how I first experienced this.

When I was in law school, I had a course on federal income taxation. One day during class I asked the law professor whether the expense of law school courses was deductible. The professor's response was that these expenses were not deductible. Actually, he went to great length to explain that there are few instances in the entire tax code as clearcut as the nondeductibility of these expenses. I must admit that this is not the answer that I wanted to hear. But wait a second. I did get the correct answer to the question I asked. Fortunately, I recognized the problem and immediately asked a follow-up question.

This follow-up question relates to a question I ask at my seminars. Basically, I was in the exact situation in which my attendees find themselves. I had asked a very well-respected tax expert an important question and I got the wrong answer. Not the wrong answer to the question, but it was not the answer I was seeking. Do you suppose that this could stop a person dead in their tracks? Certainly. The key is that we must have enough knowledge to get to the next step.

At the seminars, after I hear about what the accountants have told the attendees, I ask a new question: How many of you work for a company who will either reimburse you or pay for college courses that you take? All of a sudden, hands shoot up all over the class. I then ask those attendees whether they think that their company deducted that expense. Their answer is a resounding yes!

But wait a second, I thought that our accountant told us that we can't deduct that expense. I thought that my law professor said that these expenses are not deductible. How is it then that the company can deduct these expenses when we, as individuals, cannot? What's the difference? The difference is that those companies are business entities. As business entities, things work a little differently. Business entities can deduct many things that individuals simply cannot. This leads us to our next obstacle.

The second hurdle that people must overcome is a *lack of entities*. If you do not have a business entity, you cannot receive the benefits of business entities. Entities do you no good whatsoever if you don't have them established and operating. The accountants mentioned earlier understand this. Unfortunately, their clients do not.

The thing you need to understand is that people face two major stumbling blocks when it comes to asset protection, estate planning, and tax reduction. These are:

1. Lack of knowledge.
2. Lack of entities.

Both of these must be mastered. If you have knowledge of entities, but you don't have the actual entities, what good does this do you? Conversely, if you have entities but don't have the knowledge to effectively use the entities, how much better off are you? In essence, one cannot work without the other.

The real issue is how to overcome these areas. Which should be tackled first? That can be rather tricky, but it needs to be addressed if we plan on achieving any sort of meaningful results.

Setting up entities is easy. Anyone can go out and find an attorney, or even a company for that matter, to set up any type of entity that he or she wants. It reminds me a little bit of the real estate market. Is it difficult to purchase real estate? No. Once you go out and purchase the property, does that mean that you will automatically achieve the optimal results? Not at all. It works the same way with entities. You need to know what to do with it once you purchase it. You need the knowledge.

While knowledge alone will not make you successful, lack of knowledge can certainly make you unsuccessful. But once you come to the realization that you need the knowledge, where do you go to get it? Do colleges teach you how to actually implement strategies or do they teach theory? Remember that college course, "How to Operate Legal Entities 101?" It's not there, is it? To truly understand how to do these things, you need to learn it in a way where you can really understand.

That's what makes Trump University so special. Through their educational training programs, *anyone* can learn the secrets of the wealthy and implement them into their lives. By following a method of learning that has a centuries old track record, they provide their students with the knowledge and tools necessary to achieve unparalleled success.

The time-tested method employed by Trump University is the apprenticeship model. You've undoubtedly heard about Donald Trump's phenomenally popular show, *The Apprentice*. The challenge was that the program only chose one person to become the apprentice.

Through Trump University, this opportunity is provided for anyone who truly desires to learn the art of creating, accumulating, and preserving wealth. If you have not taken the time to learn more about the exciting programs offered through Trump University, you need to visit their web site at www.trumpuniversity.com.

One of the dynamic programs offered as part of their curriculum is the Wealth Preservation: Asset Protection Retreat. This is not a lecture setting, but an actual interactive environment where people get things done. We show you how to make sense out of legal requirements and understand technical legal jargon. It is a literal buffet of knowledge.

The workshop is a course designed as a step-by-step process for accomplishing your wealth objectives through the proper use of your legal entities. We go through how entities need to be chosen, the steps that need to be followed for taking advantage of strategies to help you protect your assets, plan your estate, and reduce your tax bill. We spend a good deal of time walking you through the flow of money from one entity to another as well so that when you leave, you are well equipped to operate your asset security system. You will learn more about the proper structuring of legal entities during your time at the boot camp than through any other period of your entire life.

The workshop is structured in a way to enable graduates to hit the ground running, fast. I'd love to be able to say that it is the best workshop of its kind, but in terms of effectiveness, it is the *only* workshop of its kind. It is a learning revolution.

The goal of this program is to provide a setting where people have the opportunity to make things happen. I learned a long time ago that you have two choices in life: You can either *wait* for things to happen, or you can go out and *make* things happen. Which type of person are you? You and you alone are in control over what type of person you are.

As I conclude this book, I'm excited. I'm excited about the opportunities available for you to go out and really make things happen. I'm excited about what you can do, not only for yourselves, but for your families. When all is said and done, you have a decision to make. You are the one responsible for what you do with what you've been presented. You can go on doing things the same old way, which will produce the same old results. Or you can do things the way million-aires do things. If you want to get different results, you must do things differently. You've got the knowledge. Now what are you going to do with it? The answer to that question makes all the difference. What's your answer?

# V

---

## RESOURCES

# DEDUCTIONS CHECKLIST

The following is a short list of other assorted expenses allowed to corporations.

Within IRS guidelines, most corporations are allowed to deduct 100% of the following expenses:

1. Advertising expenses
2. Auto expenses
3. Awards
4. Cleaning expenses
5. Depreciation and Section 179 expenses
6. Convention expenses
7. Delivery expenses
8. Dues and publication expenses
9. Foreign conventions
10. Gas and oil expenses
11. Insurance expenses
12. Legal and professional expenses
13. License fees
14. Mailer expenses
15. Meals on premises expenses
16. Office expenses
17. Pension expenses

18. Per diem meals, including incidental expenses
19. Per diem lodging, including incidental expenses
20. Postage and freight expenses
21. Trade shows and conference expenses
22. Tax expenses (including payroll, property, sales, etc.)
23. Utilities (phone, electric, gas, water, garbage, etc.)

The following are considered to be normal and necessary travel deductions:

1. Any "common carrier" fares (air, bus, rail, boat, taxi, etc.)
2. Baggage charges
3. Meals and lodging (either en route to or at the destination)
4. Rental or maintenance of an automobile
5. Reasonable cleaning and laundry expenses
6. Telephone, telegraph, computer, or fax expenses
7. Cost of transporting sample cases or display materials
8. Cost of display or conference rooms
9. Cost of maintaining and operating an airplane
10. Cost of secretarial help
11. Tips paid incident to any of the above expenses (within reason)
12. Other miscellaneous expenses related to travel

## MEDICAL EXPENSES

A major consideration for corporations these days is medical care for employees and other associated medical expenses. The IRS is quite explicit on what can be deducted in this area. For most situations, 100% of all of the following medical expenses can be deducted:

1. Accident & health insurance
2. Acupuncture

3. Adoption
4. Air conditioner (for allergy relief or other medical condition)
5. Alcoholism treatment
6. Ambulance costs
7. Birth control pills
8. Blind person's attendant (to accompany student, etc.)
9. Braille books and magazines, seeing-eye dogs, or any special education and/or educational aids for the blind
10. Capital expenditures (or home modifications for handicapped individuals, primary purpose medical care)
11. Car or van equipped to accommodate wheelchair passengers, including handicapped controls
12. Childbirth preparation classes for expectant parents
13. Chiropractors
14. Christian Science treatment
15. Clarinet & lessons (to alleviate severe teeth malocclusion)
16. Computer data bank, storage and retrieval of medical records
17. Contact lenses
18. Contraceptives
19. Cosmetic surgery
20. Crutches
21. Deaf person's hearing aids (hearing aid animals, lip-reading expenses, note taker for deaf student, computer modifications, etc.)
22. Dental fees
23. Dentures
24. Doctor's fees
25. Domestic aid
26. Drug addiction recovery
27. Drugs and prescriptions
28. Dyslexia language training
29. Electrolysis
30. Elevator to alleviate cardiac condition

31. Eye examination and prescription glasses
32. Hair transplants
33. Halfway houses (drug, alcohol rehabilitation, etc.)
34. Health club dues prescribed by physician for medical condition
35. Health Maintenance Organization (HMO)
36. Hospital care
37. Hospital services (outpatient)
38. Indian medicine man (Native Americans)
39. Insulin
40. Iron lungs
41. Laboratory fees
42. Lead paint removal
43. Legal expenses (authorization for treatment, etc.)
44. Lifetime medical care
45. Limbs (artificial)
46. Mattresses (prescribed to alleviate arthritis, etc.)
47. Nursing homes
48. Nursing services
49. Obstetrical expenses
50. Operations
51. Orthopedic shoes
52. Osteopaths
53. Oxygen equipment
54. Patterning exercises for handicapped children
55. Prosthesis
56. Psychiatric care
57. Psychologists
58. Psychotherapists
59. Reclining chairs for cardiac patients
60. Remedial reading schools (special education or handicapped)
61. Sexual dysfunction
62. Sterilization operations
63. Swimming pool (for treatment of polio or arthritis, etc.)

64. Taxicab to doctor's office
65. Telephones, equipped for deaf persons
66. Televisions (close captioned decoders, etc.)
67. Transplants
68. Vasectomies
69. Vitamins
70. Wheel chairs
71. Wigs (for alleviation of physical or mental discomfort)
72. X-Rays

# BUSINESS STRUCTURE TAX AND ASSET PROTECTION COMPARISON CHART

Use this convenient chart as a guide to first help you gain knowledge and understanding about entities, then as a tool to help you select your entity structure with your chosen team of professionals.

| Type of Business | Ownership | Limited Liability/Asset Protection | Taxation |
|---|---|---|---|
| **Sole Proprietorship** | One owner | Unlimited personal liability | Entity generally not taxed as the profits and losses are passed through to the sole proprietor ("pass-through" taxation) |
| **General Partnership** | Unlimited number of general partners allowed | Unlimited personal liability of the general partners | "Pass-through" taxation to general partners |

*(continued)*

| Type of Business | Ownership | Limited Liability/Asset Protection | Taxation |
|---|---|---|---|
| **Limited Partnership** | Unlimited number of general and limited partners allowed | Unlimited personal liability of the general partners; limited partners generally have limited liability protection | "Pass-through" taxation to the general and limited partners |
| **Limited Liability Company** | Unlimited number of "members" allowed | Generally no personal liability of the members for obligations of the business | "Pass-through" taxation to the members (unless election is made by the members to be taxed as a C corporation) |
| **C Corporation** | Unlimited number of shareholders allowed; no limit on stock classes | Generally no personal liability of the shareholders for the obligations of the corporation | Corporation taxed on its earnings at the corporate level and at corporate tax rates and the shareholders have a further tax at individual tax rates on dividends distributed ("double taxation") |
| **S Corporation** | Up to 75 shareholders allowed; only one basic class of stock allowed | Generally no personal liability of the shareholders for the obligations of the corporation | "Pass-through" taxation to the shareholders |

# State Post-Judgment (Bankruptcy) Exemptions For Homestead and Pension and Retirement Plans

This is a brief overview of the exemptions for each state. Law, and therefore, these exemptions can and do often change. Check with your professional before proceeding on any bankruptcy exemption claim to determine current law and the effects it may have on your situation.

| State | Homestead Exemption | Pensions and Retirement Plans Exemptions |
|-------|---------------------|------------------------------------------|
| **Alabama** | $5,000 per debtor, up to $10,000 | Exempt for some judges, law enforcement, state employees, and teachers. IRAs exempt for conventional, SEP and SIMPLE plans. |

*(continued)*

| State | Homestead Exemption | Pensions and Retirement Plans Exemptions |
|---|---|---|
| **Alaska** | Up to $54,000 | ERISA qualified plans exempt (minus contributions made within 120 days of filing bankruptcy). Some teacher, judicial employees, and public employees exempt. Other retirement benefits follow wage exemptions in AK. IRA exemptions for conventional, Roth, SEP and SIMPLE subject to same 120 day rule as ERISA plans. |
| **Arizona** | $100,000 limit | ERISA qualified plans exempt (minus contributions made within 120 days of filing bankruptcy). Board of Regents, state employees, public safety personnel, firefighters, police officer, and rangers are exempt. IRA exemptions for conventional, Roth, SEP and SIMPLE subject to same 120 day rule as ERISA plans. |
| **Arkansas** | *Option 1:* Unlimited for Head of Family not to exceed ¼ in town, 80 acres rural. Drops to $2,500 if ¼ to 1 acre in town, 80-160 acres rural. *Option 2:* $800 single, $1,250 married. | Firefighters, police officers, school employees & conventional, Roth, SEP and SIMPLE plans limit of $500. Nondeductible contributions to non-Roth IRAs, zero protection. |
| **California** | *Option 1:* $50,000 single, $75,000 family ($100,000 if debtor is over 65 or disabled). *Option 2:* $15,000. Unused portion may be applied to any property. | *Option 1:* County employees, county firefighters, county peace officers, and public employees. Conventional, Roth, SEP and SIMPLE are exempt. Exemption limited to amount needed for support of debtor and dependents. |

| State | Homestead Exemption | Pensions and Retirement Plans Exemptions |
| --- | --- | --- |
| | | *Option 2:* ERISA-qualified benefits, Conventional, Roth, SEP and SIMPLE plans. ALL limited to amount needed for support of debtor and dependents. |
| **Colorado** | Up to $30,000. Mobile home $6,000 | ERISA-qualified benefits. Firefighters, police officers, public employees, teachers, and veterans, and conventional, Roth, SEP and SIMPLE plans. |
| **Connecticut** | $75,000 | ERISA-qualified benefits to wage exemption. Municipal employees, teachers, state employees, probate judges and employees, veterans. Conventional, Roth, SEP and SIMPLE plans. |
| **Delaware** | None with the exception that property held by married couples as tenancy in the entirety may be exempt against debts owed by one spouse. | Various public employees. Conventional, Roth, SEP and SIMPLE plans. |
| **District of Columbia** | None with the exception that property held by married couples as tenancy in the entirety may be exempt against debts owed by one spouse. | Exemptions for teachers and judges. |
| **Florida** | Unlimited, property cannot exceed ½ acre in municipality or 160 contiguous acres rural. Property held by married couples as tenancy in the entirety may be exempt against debts owed by one spouse. | ERISA-qualified benefits. Various public employees, including profit sharing as needed for support. Conventional, Roth, SEP and SIMPLE plans. |

*(continued)*

| State | Homestead Exemption | Pensions and Retirement Plans Exemptions |
|---|---|---|
| **Georgia** | $5,000 | ERISA-qualified, public employee, and non-profit plans and Social Security benefits. All others exempt on to extent needed for support. |
| **Hawaii** | Up to 1 acre $20,000. Goes to $30,000 for married debtor or head of household over 65. | All state and some municipal plans exempt. ERISA-qualified plans and conventional, Roth, SEP and SIMPLE IRAs. Excludes contributions made within 3 years of filing. |
| **Idaho** | $50,000 | ERISA-qualified and Social Security benefits and funds of firefighters, police officers, and public employees exempted. All others exempt on to extent needed for support. |
| **Illinois** | $7,500 | ERISA-qualified benefits. Civil service and county employees, firefighters and their widows and children, disabled firefighters, general assembly members, municipal employees, police officers, state university employees and teachers exempted. Conventional, Roth, SEP and SIMPLE plans. |
| **Indiana** | $7,500. Property held by married couples as tenancy in the entirety may be exempt against debts owed by one spouse. | Funds of firefighters, police officers, sheriffs, public employees, and state teachers exempted. Conventional, SEP and SIMPLE IRAs. Non-deductible contributions not protected. |

| State | Homestead Exemption | Pensions and Retirement Plans Exemptions |
|---|---|---|
| **Iowa** | Unlimited. Cannot exceed ½ acre in town or 40 acres elsewhere. | Funds of firefighters, police officers, and public employees exempted. Other pensions exempt if needed for support. |
| **Kansas** | $50,000 | ERISA-qualified benefits. Funds exempt for city officials in cities with populations of 120,000-200,000, firefighters, police officers, government employees, and state school employees exempted. Conventional, Roth, SEP and SIMPLE IRA plans. |
| **Kentucky** | $5,000 | Funds of firefighters, police officers, teachers, state employees, and county government employees exempted. Other pensions exempt if needed for support. Conventional, Roth, SEP and SIMPLE plans (minus contributions made within 120 days of filing bankruptcy). |
| **Louisiana** | $15,000 up to 160 acres | ERISA-qualified plans. Conventional, SEP and SIMPLE IRAs, KEOUGHs and other qualified plans exempt to equivalent as tax exemption (minus contributions made within 1 year of filing bankruptcy). |
| **Maine** | $12,500, minors present in residence $25,000, 60 or disabled $60,000. Joint debtors can double exemption. | ERISA-qualified plans. Funds of legislators, judges, and state employees, conventional, Roth, SEP and SIMPLE IRA plans exempted to amounts necessary for support of debtor and dependents. |

*(continued)*

| State | Homestead Exemption | Pensions and Retirement Plans Exemptions |
|---|---|---|
| **Maryland** | None with the exception that property held by married couples as tenancy in the entirety may be exempt against debts owed by one spouse. | ERISA-qualified plans. Funds of teachers, state employees, and deceased Baltimore police officers exempted. Conventional, Roth, SEP and SIMPLE IRA plans exempted, but limited to tax-deductible contributions for non-Roth IRAs. |
| **Massachusetts** | $100,000, $200,000 if over 65 or disabled. Property held by married couples as tenancy in the entirety may be exempt against debts owed by one spouse. | ERISA-qualified plans. Public employees and savings bank employees' plans exempt. Conventional, Roth, SEP and SIMPLE IRA plans exempted, but with limitations to contributions 5 years prior to filing bankruptcy. |
| **Michigan** | $3,500 not to exceed 1 lot urban or 40 acres rural. Property held as tenancy in the entirety may be exempt against debts owed by one spouse. | ERISA-qualified plans. Funds of firefighters, police officers, legislators, state employees, and public school employees exempted. Conventional, Roth, SEP and SIMPLE IRA plans exempted, but limited to tax-deductible contributions for non-Roth IRAs, and minus contributions made within 120 days of filing for bankruptcy. |
| **Minnesota** | $200,000 ($500,000 for property used primarily as agricultural) not to exceed ½ acre urban or 160 acres rural. | ERISA-qualified plans limited to current value of $51,000. Funds exempt for public and state employees. Conventional, Roth, SEP and SIMPLE IRA plans with same limitations on value as ERISA plans. |

| State | Homestead Exemption | Pensions and Retirement Plans Exemptions |
|---|---|---|
| **Mississippi** | $75,000 not to exceed 160 acres | ERISA-qualified plans limited to contributions made within 1 year of filing bankruptcy. Funds of firefighters, police officers, teachers, and state employees exempted. |
| **Missouri** | $8,000 (mobile homes $1000) | ERISA-qualified plans. Funds exempt for city employees in cities with populations of 100,000 or more, public officers and employees, firefighters, police officers, highway and transportation employees, teachers, and state employees exempted. Conventional, Roth, SEP and SIMPLE IRA plans (minus contributions made within 3 years of filing). |
| **Montana** | $60,000 | ERISA-qualified plans. Funds exempt for all public employees. Conventional, Roth, SEP and SIMPLE IRA plans (ERISA-qualified and IRAs are minus contributions made within 1 year of filing which are in excess of 15% of income for that year). Additional restrictions for SEP and SIMPLE IRAs may apply. |
| **Nebraska** | $12,500, cannot exceed two urban lots or 160 acres rural | ERISA-qualified plans as needed for support. Funds for county, state, and school employees exempted. Military disability benefits to $2,000. Conventional, Roth, SEP and SIMPLE IRA plans (excluding plans established within 2 years of filing) are limited to amounts reasonable and necessary for support of debtor and dependents. |

*(continued)*

| State | Homestead Exemption | Pensions and Retirement Plans Exemptions |
|---|---|---|
| **Nevada** | $125,000 | ERISA-qualified plans and conventional, SEP and SIMPLE IRAs all up to $500,000. Funds exempt for public employees. |
| **New Hampshire** | $30,000 | Funds exempt for all public employees' federal pensions (limited to benefits accruing). Funds for firefighters, police officers, and public employees. |
| **New Jersey** | None | ERISA-qualified plans. Funds exempt for all public employees. Conventional, Roth, education, SEP and SIMPLE IRA plans. |
| **New Mexico** | $30,000. If jointly owned, may double. | Funds exempt for public school employees. |
| **New York** | $10,000. Husband and wife may double. | ERISA-qualified benefits as needed for support. State employees and village police officers' public retirement benefits exempted. Conventional, Roth, SEP and SIMPLE IRA plans (minus contributions made within 90 days of filing). |
| **North Carolina** | $10,000 | Funds exempt for firefighters and rescue squad workers, legislators, law enforcement officers, municipal city and county employees, teachers, and state employees. Conventional, Roth, SEP and SIMPLE IRA plans (but subject to statutory and consensual liens). |

| State | Homestead Exemption | Pensions and Retirement Plans Exemptions |
|---|---|---|
| **North Dakota** | $80,000 | Funds exempt for disabled veteran's benefits and public employees' pensions. ERISA-qualified plans and conventional, Roth, SEP and SIMPLE IRA plans up to $100,000 per plan ($200,000 maximum unless necessary for support of debtor or dependents). |
| **Ohio** | $5,000. Property held as tenancy in the entirety may be exempt against debts owed by one spouse. | ERISA-qualified plans. Funds for firefighters' and police officers' death benefits and pensions, public employees, state highway patrol employees and volunteer firefighters' dependents. Conventional, Roth, education, SEP and SIMPLE IRA plans. |
| **Oklahoma** | Unlimited. Cannot exceed ¼ acre. If exceeds ¼ acre, limited to $5,000 per 1 acre urban, 160 acres rural. | ERISA-qualified plans. Funds for public employees, law enforcement employees, teachers, county employees, and disabled veterans. Conventional, SEP and SIMPLE IRA plans exempted, but limited to tax-deductible contributions only. |
| **Oregon** | $25,000 ($33,000 for joint owners). If land is not owned limit is $23,000 ($30,000 joint). Property not to exceed 1 block in town or 160 acres rural. | ERISA-qualified plans. Funds exempt for public employees or officers and school district employees. Conventional, Roth, SEP and SIMPLE IRA plans exempt. |

*(continued)*

| State | Homestead Exemption | Pensions and Retirement Plans Exemptions |
|---|---|---|
| **Pennsylvania** | None. Except that property held as tenancy in the entirety may be exempt against debts owed by one spouse. | ERISA-qualified plans. Funds exempt for city, county and municipal employees, police officers, and public school employees. Private retirement benefits exempt only if clause prohibits proceeds being used to pay beneficiary's creditors, to the extent tax-deferred, limited to $15,000 per year deposited, and minus deposits within 1 year of filing. Conventional, Roth, SEP and SIMPLE IRA plans exempt with same limitations as above. |
| **Rhode Island** | None | ERISA-qualified plans. Funds exempt for all public employees. Conventional, Roth, SEP and SIMPLE IRA plans exempted, but limited to tax-deductible contributions for non-Roth IRAs. |
| **South Carolina** | $5,000 (joint owners may double) | ERISA-qualified plans. Funds exempt Social Security and miscellaneous state and local employee retirement systems. Conventional, Roth, SEP and SIMPLE IRA plans exempt, but limited to payments, not balance in plans. Limitations on SEP and SIMPLE plans. |
| **South Dakota** | Unlimited with square footage minimums and not to exceed 1 acre urban and 160 acres rural. | Funds exempt for public and city employees. Maximum of $250,00 for all plans. Conventional, SEP and SIMPLE IRA plans with same limitations on value as above plans. |

| State | Homestead Exemption | Pensions and Retirement Plans Exemptions |
|---|---|---|
| **Tennessee** | $5,000 ($7,500 jointly owned). Property held as tenancy in the entirety may be exempt against debts owed by one spouse. | ERISA-qualified plans. Funds exempt for public employees, state and local government employees, and teachers. Conventional, SEP and SIMPLE IRA plans exempt. |
| **Texas** | Unlimited. Cannot exceed 1 acre urban or 100 acres (200 for families) elsewhere. | ERISA-qualified government or church benefits. Funds exempt for county and district employees, firefighters, judges (KEOUGHs tax-deferred amounts only), law enforcement officers' survivors, municipal employees, police officers, state employees, and teachers. Conventional, Roth, SEP and SIMPLE IRA plans exempt, but limited to tax-deductible contributions for non-Roth IRAs. |
| **Utah** | $10,000 (joint owners may double) | ERISA-qualified plans. Funds exempt for public employees or officers and school district employees. Conventional, Roth, SEP and SIMPLE IRA plans exempt for contribution made 1 year prior to filing. |
| **Vermont** | $75,000. Property held as tenancy in the entirety may be exempt against debts owed by one spouse. | Municipal and state employees and teachers funds exempt. Conventional, Roth, SEP and SIMPLE IRA plans exempt for contribution made 1 year prior to filing and limited to tax-deductible contributions for non-Roth IRAs. Exemption limited to $5,000 if court action is for child support. |

*(continued)*

| State | Homestead Exemption | Pensions and Retirement Plans Exemptions |
|---|---|---|
| **Virginia** | $5,000 (spouses may double) | ERISA-qualified plans limited to $17,500 per year. Exempt for judges and city, town, county, and state employees. Conventional, SEP and SIMPLE IRA plans with same limitations on value as above plans and with no protection for contributions made in current and two previous years. |
| **Washington** | $30,000 | ERISA-qualified plans. Funds exempt for all city employees, volunteer firefighters, state patrol officers, and public employees. Conventional, Roth, education, SEP and SIMPLE IRA plans exempted. |
| **West Virginia** | $15,000 | ERISA-qualified plans. Funds exempt for public employees. Conventional, Roth, education, SEP and SIMPLE IRA plans limited to amount necessary for support of debtor and dependents. Additional limitations on some SEP and SIMPLE plans. |
| **Wisconsin** | $40,000 | Private or public retirement funds generally exempt for certain municipal employees; firefighters and police officers in cities with populations over 100,000; military pensions and public employees. Conventional, Roth, education, SEP and SIMPLE IRA plans limited to amount necessary for support of debtor and dependents. May also be subject to many different types of claims and liens. |

| State | Homestead Exemption | Pensions and Retirement Plans Exemptions |
| --- | --- | --- |
| **Wyoming** | $10,000 (house trailer $6,000). Joint owners may double. | Private or public retirement funds and accounts for criminal investigators, highway officers, county employees, firefighters, police officers, public employees, and game and fish wardens. For firefighters and police officers, limited to payments being received. |

# Glossary:
## Terms That the Wealthy
## Know That You Must Learn

**Accumulated earnings tax**   A penalty tax charged against a corporation that retains an excessive amount of profits beyond the reasonable needs of its business, rather than distributing those profits to its owners. An LLC that is taxed as a partnership does not face this problem.

**Adjusted gross income (AGI)**   All your income from whatever source (wages, rents, dividends, profits from a business, and so forth) less certain deductions (trade or business expenses, depreciation on rental property, allowable losses from sales of property, alimony payments, and so forth). Adjusted gross income is important for calculating the amount of medical expenses and casualty losses that you can deduct. A modified version of AGI is used in determining how much Social Security is taxed. The $25,000 special allowance to deduct rental expenses when you actively participate is based on modified AGI, which is AGI increased by any passive activity losses, certain Social Security payments, and individual retirement account (IRA) deductions. This is important in assessing the value to an investment in the low-income housing credit.

**Administrator**   Person appointed by a court to administer and settle the estate of a person who dies without a will, or the estate of a person who has a will but the appointed executor cannot serve; also called a personal representative.

**Alternative minimum tax (AMT)**   Calculated by starting with your taxable income according to the regular tax rules. Add certain tax preference items and adjustments required by the AMT. Only certain itemized deductions are allowed. Next, subtract any exemption amount. The result is multiplied by either a 26 percent or 28 percent rate for individuals. If the amount due exceeds the tax you owe under the regular tax system then you must pay the larger AMT.

**Asset protection**   The process of taking steps to minimize the risk of creditors or other claimants being able to reach your assets. This can include setting up a different entity, such as an LLC, for each property or business. Thus, if one particular property is subject to a suit (e.g., a tenant is hurt on one rental property), the claimant is limited to the assets from that particular property or entity. This can prevent a domino effect against your other assets. An LLC, just like a limited partnership, offers important benefits in the area of asset protection.

**Assets**   Anything owned with monetary value. This includes both real and personal property.

**Attorney-in-fact**   An agent who is given written authorization by you to take certain actions on your behalf.

**Basis**   Taxpayer's investment for tax purposes.

**Beneficiary**   Person for whom a trust is managed and who eventually receives the trust corpus after the death of the trust grantor. In another context, the beneficiary is the recipient of life insurance proceeds, benefit plans, or gifts in a will.

**Bequest**   Property transferred under a will.

**Calendar year**   The accounting year beginning January 1 and ending December 31.

**Capital expenditure**   A payment to buy, build, or improve an asset (property you own) that lasts for more than one year. Capital expenditures generally can't be deducted in the year paid. Instead, they must usually be added to your investment (adjusted basis) in the asset and then written off (depreciated) over a period of time.

**Capital gain**   The gain from selling a capital asset. The gain usually equals the amount realized or the selling price less your investment (adjusted tax basis) in the property. Capital gains receive favorable tax treatment in that the maximum rate is set at 28 percent while the maximum tax rate on ordinary income is 39.6 percent. Capital losses can only be deducted in any year up to the amount of capital gains plus $3,000.

**Capitalize**   To add expenses that are not deductible to a person's investment (adjusted basis) in a property.

**C corporation**   A corporation that pays federal taxes on its net income. (See **S corporation.**)

**Centralized management**   One of four characteristics that distinguish an entity taxed as a partnership (flow-through income and loss to the owner) and an association taxable as a corporation (the corporate entity pays tax and then the owner pays tax on distributions received, see **Double taxation.**). Centralized management is a corporate (not partnership) characteristic.

**Certificate or Articles of Incorporation**   The document that creates a corporation according to the laws of the state. This must be filed with and approved by the state.

**Charging order**   A statutorily created means for a creditor of a judgment debtor who is a partner of others to reach the debtor's beneficial interest in the partnership without risking dissolution of the partnership.

**Charitable remainder trust (CRT)**   The donation of property or money to a charity when the donor reserves the right to use the property or receive income from it for a specified number of years (or for life, or for the duration of the life of a second person such as a spouse). When the agreed period is over, the property belongs to the charitable organization.

**Closely held business**  A family business or a business owned by relatively few individuals.

**Codicil**  An amendment to a will. The requirements for execution of a codicil are the same as for execution of a will. Therefore, if you are planning to make extensive changes to your will, it is generally better to execute a new will rather than amend an old will with codicils.

**Continuity of life**  One of the four characteristics that distinguishes an entity taxed as a partnership and an association taxed as a corporation.

**Contribution**  Property transferred to an LLC in exchange for a membership interest in the LLC. This type of transfer is often referred to as a contribution of property to the LLC. Special tax rules affect this transfer. Generally, you do not have a taxable gain on the contribution of property to an LLC in exchange for a membership interest.

**Corporation**  A business formed and authorized by law to act as a single entity. Although it may be owned by one or more persons (called shareholders), it is legally endowed with rights and responsibilities and has a life of its own independent of the owners and operators. The owners are not personally liable for debts or obligations of the corporation. Corporations can be S corporations or C corporations.

**Decedent**  A person who has died. A decedent's assets are disposed of by will, or if no will exists, by the intestacy laws of the decedent's state.

**Deferral of estate tax**  A provision of estate tax law. Where a sufficient portion of your estate comprises assets in a closely held and active business, your estate may qualify to pay the estate tax attributable to these assets over approximately a 14-year period instead of within nine months of death. The fact that a business interest is owned by an entity does not necessarily disqualify it for this favorable estate tax provision.

**Deferral of income**   A common tax planning technique used around December 31. By not recognizing income until the next year, the taxpayer may postpone payment on the income for another full year. Examples of income deferral include delaying the sale of stocks or property until January, selling property on the installment method, not receiving cash until the next year, and so forth.

**Depreciation**   The writing off an asset's cost over its useful life or using other methods prescribed by tax laws. Depreciation is based on the idea that property wears down over time from exposure to the elements, physical wear and tear from use, and so forth. Depreciation of assets held by your LLC or partnership are passed to your personal tax return and deducted there as a part of the results you realize in that given tax year from your LLC or partnership.

**Descendant**   A person who is a relative in a direct line from another person, also called issue.

**Discount**   A discount on the value of a gift of a minority (less than controlling) and/or lack of marketability interest in an LLC may sometimes be claimed. This can enable the donor to give a greater percentage interest in the LLC as a gift in any year under the annual exclusion without, for example, using any of the donor's unified credit.

**Dissolution**   Formal statutory liquidation, termination, and winding up of a business entity.

**Distribution**   The parceling out of profits or other assets to members/owners of a legal entity. As a member/owner, you may receive distributions of cash or even property. Depending on the entity, however, your tax results may not be limited to the amount you receive as a distribution. In a pass-through taxation entity, you are taxed on your pro rata portion of LLC income or loss.

**Distributive share**   The share of property inherited by a beneficiary when a decedent dies without a will. For example, if the person who dies without a will has no surviving spouse and two surviving children, in most states, the children divide the estate equally. This would be each child's distributive share.

**Donee**   A person who receives a gift.

**Donor**   A person who makes a gift.

**Double taxation**   Occurs when corporations pay tax on corporate profits and shareholders pay income tax on dividend or distributive income.

**Durable Power of Attorney**   A document in which you grant certain people (your attorneys-in-fact) the authority to handle your financial matters.

**Election**   In accounting, the choice of a particular method for calculating taxes. The tax laws provide for optional treatment of many items. Often the taxpayer must make an election (usually by filing a statement or checking a box on the tax return) as to which method will be used. Legal entities, as separate tax reporting entities, must make their own tax elections.

**Employer identification number (EIN)**   A number issued by the federal government to identify a business for tax purposes. In a sole proprietorship, your Social Security number serves as your EIN.

**Estate tax**   A tax that may be due on the death of a taxpayer, as a result of the transfer of wealth to family and others. Exclusions are provided for transfers to the taxpayer's spouse, charities, and so forth. The tax rate for the estate tax can reach as high as 55 percent. A once-in-a-lifetime credit is permitted that enables you to pass property worth up to $600,000 to others (not including spouses) without having to pay a federal estate tax.

**Estimated tax**   Income taxes paid by certain individuals on a quarterly basis to avoid underpayment penalties. Your expected income (or loss) from your investments must be considered in making these calculations.

**Executor**   An individual or institution named in a will to administer the estate of the person making the will. The executor legally steps into the shoes of the decedent and represents the estate in probate court. In some states, the executor is also called the *personal representative*.

**Fair market value**   The price at which an item can be sold at the present time between two unrelated people, neither under compulsion to buy or sell. Where a gift is made of an interest in an entity, it must be valued at its fair market value. This may, in the case of an LLC, be permitted to reflect a minority (lack of control) and/or lack of marketability discount.

**Family limited partnership (FLP)**   A limited partnership owned by a family for purposes of transferring some of the value of the business or real estate to the younger generation and possibly involving them in the management of the business as well.

**Fiduciary**   A person having the legal duty to act primarily for the benefit of the principal. The fiduciary must act in the strictest confidence and trust. A trustee or an agent would be a fiduciary acting on behalf of the principal.

**50–50 rule**   A rule governing estate taxation of jointly held property between husband and wife. Under this rule, only half the value of property owned by tenancies by the entirety or joint tenancies with rights of survivorship are included in the gross estate of the first spouse to die, no matter how much or how little either spouse contributed.

**Fiscal year**  A tax year (12-month period) other than the calendar year used by a particular taxpayer. Some entities, such as LLCs and LPs are subject to limitations on when they can use a tax year other than the calendar year.

**Foreign partnership**  A partnership formed in one state or country but conducting some or all of its business in another state or country.

**Formal will**  A typed or printed will that must be witnessed and acknowledged by the testator to the effect that he is executing his or her will.

**Free transferability**  The ability to transfer ownership interest without the consent of other owners. A key characteristic in distinguishing the taxation of an LLC as a partnership or as an association taxable as a corporation. Where interests in your LLC can be freely transferred without restriction, it is more like a corporation than a partnership.

The LLC's operating agreement could include restrictions so that, for example, the manager or 75 percent of the members may have to approve a transfer. Also, where the transfer is not approved, the person acquiring the interest is merely a substitute assignee and not an actual member. Thus, certain important attributes of ownership may not be passed where the approval process is not obtained.

**General partner**  An owner of a partnership who is personally liable for all partnership debts and may be permitted to participate in the management of the partnership. Every limited partnership must have at least one general partner. Often this general partner is a corporation, which avoids any one individual being personally liable.

**General partnership**  A partnership that has only general partners. This is the most common way for a few friends or investors to put their money together to buy a rental property or simple business. All partners share equally in contributions, distributions, and responsibilities. In a general partnership, all partners are personally liable, without limit, for all partnership debts.

**Generation-skipping transfer (GST) tax**   A tax generally assessed on transfers to grandchildren, great-grandchildren, and so on.

**Gift**   For purposes of taxation, the transfer of property without the donor receiving something of equal value in return. The federal government assesses a transfer tax where the value of the gift exceeds the annual exclusion and the unified credit equivalent is exhausted.

**Gift splitting**   A married couple's agreement to treat a gift made by one of them to a third party as having been made one-half by each. This lowers the gift tax rate and, in many cases, significantly reduces, or even eliminates, any gift tax.

**Gift tax**   A tax that may be due when you give property or other assets away. You are allowed to give away up to the annual exclusion amount per person (to any number of people) in any year without the tax applying. Above the annual exclusion amount, you have a once-in-a-lifetime exclusion that permits you to give away a limited amount of property to any individuals other than a spouse without paying any gift tax. The gift tax and the estate tax are coordinated (unified) so that the exclusion is only available once between them.

**Grantor**   The person who establishes a trust and transfers assets to it, also called a *trustor* or *settlor*.

**Gross estate**   The total value of the assets you own at death (less liabilities) that are included in your estate. The value is determined at the date of your death or as of the alternate valuation date, which is six months following the date of death.

**Gross income**   All your earnings from all sources including wages, rents, royalties, dividends, interest, and so forth.

**Gross value**   The value of an estate before debts or encumbrances are paid. Probate fees are generally calculated on the gross value of the estate. For instance, if your estate consists of your residence with a market value of $200,000 and a mortgage of $125,000, probate fees would be based on the gross value of your estate, which in this case would be $200,000.

**Guardian**   Someone who is legally responsible for the care and well-being of another person. A guardian is generally nominated in the case of a minor or when a person becomes disabled or incompetent.

**Heirs**   The persons who receive your assets following your death.

**Holographic will**   This is a will entirely written, dated, and signed by the person in his or her own handwriting.

**Improvements**   Payments for additions or betterments to property that last more than a year and must thus be added to your investment (capitalized as part of your basis) in the property.

**Incapacitated or incompetent person**   Someone who is unable to manage his own affairs due to physical or mental impairment. An incompetent person cannot enter into a contract nor can he set up a trust, or appoint an agent to act on his behalf. In the absence of any suitable planning for disability, a court has to be petitioned for the appointment of a guardian.

**Inheritance tax**   A tax on the right to receive property from a deceased person. Inheritance tax is measured by the share passing to each beneficiary.

**Insolvency**   A financial condition that exists when business liabilities exceed assets and creditors cannot be paid.

**Installment sale**   A sale where taxable gain is recognized over a number of years as payment is received for the property sold. If you are a dealer in property, you can't use the installment method. If you are a dealer in real estate, for example, but have a single property held as an investment, segregating that different property in an LLC may help support your position with the IRS that the particular property is different from those in which you are a dealer.

**Insurance trust**   An irrevocable trust established to own your insurance policies and thereby prevent them from being included in your estate. Insurance trusts are often used in planning for the tax interest in closely held businesses and nonliquid assets such as real estate.

**Intangible assets or property**   Property that you hold that has no intrinsic value but merely represents the value of underlying assets. Stocks and bonds are examples of this.

**Interest**   Entitlement to or being a permissible recipient of either the income or principal in a legal entity or asset. A reference to your ownership of a portion of an LLC. Also known as *membership interest*.

**Inter vivos trust**   A trust established by an individual during his or her lifetime, also known as a *living trust*. Such a trust can be either revocable or irrevocable. This is the opposite of a testamentary trust.

**Intestate**   Dying without a valid will. Also a person who dies with a will but fails to dispose of all his property is referred to as having left property by intestacy.

**Irrevocable**   A trust that cannot be changed after you've established it. This is an essential characteristic to have assets that you give to the trust removed from your estate.

**Issue**   All descendants of a particular person. The term includes children, grandchildren, and other direct descendants.

**Joint tenancy with right of survivorship**   Two or more persons holding title to a property jointly with equal rights during their lifetime with the survivor to receive the entire property. In other words, death of a joint owner automatically transfers ownership of the property to the surviving joint tenants. Joint tenancy supersedes any provisions contained in your will. Joint tenancy is different from tenancy in common.

**Judgment creditor**   A creditor or other plaintiff who has obtained a court-ordered judgment against a debtor.

GLOSSARY

**Judgment debtor**  A person who has a court-ordered judgment against him.

**Kiddie tax**  Unearned income (dividends, rents, interest, and so forth) of a child under age 18. This income is taxed to the child at the parent's highest tax rate. This tax makes family tax planning much more difficult.

**Lease**  A legal contract permitting one party to use property owned by another, usually for the payment of periodic rent.

**Liability**  The condition of being responsible for possible or actual loss, penalty, evil, expense, or burden; the state of being bound or obliged by law or justice to do, pay, or make good something.

**Limited liability**  The characteristic of an entity that can be sued, but whose owners generally cannot be held personally liable for debts or losses of the entity. The classic limited liability entity is the corporation.

**Limited liability company (LLC)**  An entity formed under your state's LLC statute that, like a corporation, has the legal characteristic of limited liability and that also may qualify to be treated for tax purposes as a partnership.

**Limited partner**  A partner (owner) in a limited partnership who contributes capital or property to the partnership but who cannot participate in the management of the partnership's business and who is not liable for partnership debts.

**Limited partnership**  A partnership with at least one general partner who has complete personal liability and control over the partnership and any number of limited partners with limited personal liability but no control or management over the business.

**Liquidation**  Termination and winding up of an entity, such as an LLC, corporation, revocable trust, and so on. A final tax return must be filed with the IRS and with state and local tax authorities.

**Manager**   The individual or entity charged with managing an LLC, making key decisions, and so forth. The Articles of Organization may specify who is to be the manager. The operating agreement should provide details as to the scope of the powers of the manager, liability for acts, replacement, and so forth. The manager may or may not be a member of the LLC.

**Marital deduction**   An exemption from the estate tax for an unlimited amount of assets that can be transferred from one spouse to the other. This approach is too often used as the beginning and end of estate planning.

**Member**   An owner of part (or in some states all) of an LLC. A member in an LLC is analogous to a shareholder in a corporation or a partner in a partnership. Some key characteristics and rights of a member may be set forth in the LLC's Articles of Organization. An Operating Agreement should be drafted that specifically states a member's rights, liability, and so forth.

**Minority discount**   A discount based on the concept that no person would pay as much for a noncontrolling interest in an asset such as an LLC as for a controlling interest (i.e., more than 50 percent). If you make a gift of an interest in your LLC to your child, the value of the gift must be determined to ascertain whether a gift tax is due. The gift is generally valued at its fair market value. However, this value may be reduced by a minority discount.

**Operating Agreement**   The written contract between all the owners (members) of an LLC. An LLC Operating Agreement is analogous to a corporation's Shareholders' Agreement and a partnership's Partnership Agreement. This agreement should address in detail the rights and obligations of members and managers. It should contain buy out provisions in the event of the death or disability of a member. Tax issues should be addressed: Naming a tax matters partner and defining his or her rights, allocating tax benefits, and so forth. It is almost always a mistake to think that avoiding an Operating Agreement saves costs.

**Ordinary and necessary expense** With reference to taxes, a requirement for deductibility. For payments to be deductible, they must be ordinary and necessary expenses of your trade or business. Extravagant or personal expenses are not deductible.

**Ordinary income** Income or gain from selling property that is not a capital asset. Ordinary income is taxed at rates of up to 39.6 percent, which is less favorable than capital gains rates of a maximum 28 percent. There is often an advantage for taxpayers to realize capital gains rather than ordinary income.

**Organizational expenses** Costs incurred to set up a business (such as an LP, LLC, or corporation), that can't currently be deducted. Instead these costs can be written off (amortized) over 60 months beginning with the date your business, partnership, or corporation begins to conduct an active business. Be sure to discuss this with your accountant when organizing your legal entity.

**Partnership** A syndicate, joint venture, group, or other arrangement, in which two or more investors join their money and skills to carry out a business as co-owners and to earn a profit. A partnership is generally treated as a flow-through (conduit) so that each partner reports his or her share of partnership income or loss on his or her personal tax return. The partnership files a Form 1065 with the IRS but does not pay any tax. An election is available to avoid being taxed as a partnership. See also **General partnership** and **Limited partnership**.

**Partnership interest** The ownership of interest in a partnership. In addition to limited or general partnerships, since most LLCs are taxed as partnerships, your ownership of the LLC (your membership interest) is treated for tax purposes as a partnership interest.

**Passive income** A type of income. The passive income and loss rules divide income into three types: (1) active (wages, income from and active business), (2) passive (income earned from rental property or as a limited partner investor), and (3) portfolio (dividends and interest on stocks and bonds). Passive losses (tax losses from rental property or from investments made as a limited partner) can only be applied to offset passive income. If you qualify as actively participating in a real estate rental activity, you may be able to deduct up to $25,000 of your passive tax losses against any income without regard to this limitation. Your interest in an LLC is treated as generating passive or active income depending on the nature of the LLC's business and assets, as well as your involvement.

**Passive loss**  Tax losses from rental real estate properties (e.g., as a result of depreciation write offs) or from investments as a limited partner. Passive losses can generally only be used to offset passive income.

**Pass-through tax status**  A tax method for certain business entities whereby the profits and losses of the business are reported on the owner's personal tax return.

**Personal property**  Furniture, equipment, and other movable property and assets. Buildings and land are not personal property, they are *real property*. Real property and tangible personal property are generally subject to probate in the state in which they are located on your death. If you are domiciled (permanently reside) in another state, you can avoid ancillary probate in the state where personal or real property is located by transferring those tangible assets into a legal entity (such as a trust, corporation, or an LLC) that may afford some estate planning benefits.

**Pour-over will**  As the name implies, a pour-over will is used to transfer property to a living trust that was not transferred to the trust during the lifetime of the settlor. People often fund their living trusts with the majority of the assets that they own. However, any residual assets could be transferred to the trust after the settlor's death through a pour-over will. All of the assets contained in the living trust prior to the settlor's death escape probate. However, the assets poured over through the will must go through probate. The advantage of the pour-over will is that it provides for a uniform distribution of your property under the provisions of one single, legal instrument, namely the *living trust.*

**Power of attorney** This is a legal document giving another person, known as agent or attorney in fact, the full legal authority to act in your behalf in your absence. A power of attorney loses its validity in the event the principal becomes disabled or dies. Most states, however, permit a durable power of attorney, which remains valid through the disability or incompetency of the principal. A durable power of attorney can be used in conjunction with a living trust by allowing the agent to transfer any property that wasn't transferred prior to the disability of the settlor of the trust.

**Present interest** A reference to a gift that the beneficiary can enjoy immediately. A gift must be of present interest to qualify for the annual gift tax exclusion.

**Probate** This is a judicial proceeding used for transferring a decedent's assets to his legal heirs. It is a process of administering a deceased person's estate. Unless the estate is small, a will generally has to be probated. In the absence of a will, the probate court appoints an administrator to handle the decedent's estate. All questions concerning the disposition and the rights of heirs and creditors are determined through probate. The actual probate process includes having the will recognized by the court (often called the Surrogate's Court), and having the person designated in the will (personal administrator or executor) officially empowered to act (often by issuance of documents called letters testamentary). Ancillary probate is probate in a state other than the state in which you reside. Ancillary probate and the attendant fees and time delays can be avoided, in many instances, through the proper use of legal entities.

**Probate guardianship** A judicial proceeding during which a guardian may be appointed by a probate court to manage the financial affairs of a disabled or incompetent person or of a minor. The guardian appointed by the court is required to make accounting of his actions to the court.

**Pro rata share**   A simple (from an economic perspective) LLC arrangement in which each member shares pro rata in the income, expenses, profits, and losses of the LLC. In a more complex arrangement, special allocations of income, expenses, profits, and losses may be used instead.

**Registered agent**   A person designated in accordance with state law to receive notices directed to a business entity.

**Residuary**   The assets remaining in your estate after all specific transfers of property are made and all expenses are paid. When a pour-over will is used, the residuary is poured into your living trust. (See **Pour-over will**.)

**Revocable trust**   A trust that can be amended or terminated by its creator. As opposed to an irrevocable trust, a revocable trust generally has no tax benefits.

**S corporation**   A corporation whose income is generally taxed only to its shareholders, thus avoiding a corporate level tax. An S corporation must meet numerous restrictions to qualify for this tax treatment. An LLC is not subject to these restrictions and when structured to be taxed as a partnership (as most are), it can have the same tax benefits of an S corporation with much greater ease and flexibility. (See also **Pass-through tax status**.)

**Section 2503(c) trust**   A special trust established for minor children that permits gifts to it to qualify for the annual $10,000 gift tax exclusion even though they are not gifts of a present interest. Gifts of legal entity shares or interests can be made outright to a child or in trust for the child for even greater control. Where the gifts are made in trust, the 2503(c) rules can be important.

**Securities**   Stocks, bonds, notes, convertible debentures, warrants, or other documents that represent a share in a company or a debt owed by a company or government entity.

**Service business** A business that sells service or advice instead of a tangible product.

**Shareholders** Owners of a corporation; may also be called stockholders. This is analogous to owners of an LLC, who are called members.

**Silent partner** A dormant or limited partner; one whose name does not appear in the firm and who takes no active part in the business, but who has an interest in the concern and shares the profits.

**Sole proprietorships** A business run by one person that is owned and operated in the absence of a formal business entity (no corporation, partnership, or LLC). Advantages of using a sole proprietorship are simplicity, no additional cost, and one level of tax. The tremendous disadvantage is that the owner has unlimited personal liability. An LLC is not an option for a sole proprietor in some states where at least two members are required to form an LLC. The solution may be to make a spouse, child, partner, or business associate as a nominal owner (member).

**State statutes** Laws created and codified by a state legislative body.

**Tangible assets or property** Real or personal property; assets with physical value, as distinguished from intangible property.

**Taxable income** Cash or certain economic benefits that you receive or have control over (constructive receipt) that are subject to tax (because no exclusion is allowed for them).

**Tax basis** A formula for determining the taxable value of property. The amount invested to purchase property, plus the cost of capital improvements, less depreciation is the adjusted tax basis in that property. Your adjusted tax basis is the amount used to determine any taxable gain or loss on your sale of any asset.

**Tenancy in common** A form of ownership of property by two or more persons. Different from joint tenancy or tenancy by the entirety.

On the death of a tenant in common, ownership transfers to that person's heirs, not to the surviving owners.

**Testamentary trust**   A trust created in a will that does not come into existence until after the testator's death.

**Testate**   The status of having a properly executed will at the time of one's death.

**Testator**   The person who makes a will.

**Trust**   A legal contract whereby a person or institution (trustee) holds or manages property for the benefit of someone else (beneficiary). The terms of the trust are generally governed by a contract that the grantor prepares when establishing the trust.

**Trustee**   An individual or institution holding and managing property for the benefit of someone else as per instructions contained in the trust agreement.

**Unified credit**   Permits an individual to gift (during life and death) up to $600,000 of assets to any person or persons without paying any federal estate or gift taxes on this amount. There have been many proposals to increase or decrease this amount.

**Uniform Gifts (Transfers) to Minors Act (UGMA or UTMA)** A method to hold property for the benefit of another person, such as your child, which is similar to a trust, but which is governed by state law. It is simpler and much cheaper to establish and administer than a trust, but it is far less flexible.

**Uniform Limited Liability Company Act (ULLCA)**   A set of regulations proposed for LLCs. Many states have or will eventually enact some version of this. Be careful not to assume that any particular state follows the ULLCA in all respects. There are often subtle, if not significant differences between the statutes in different states even where those statutes are based on the same uniform act.

**Uniform Limited Partnership Act (ULPA)**  A set of regulations for limited partnerships adopted with some modifications by most of the 50 states, the District of Columbia, and several U.S. territories.

**Uniform Partnership Act (UPA)**  A set of regulations for partnerships adopted with some modifications by most of the 50 states, the District of Columbia, and several U.S. territories.

**Valuation discount**  One type of discount on the value of an asset. For example, the value of an asset given to a child may be less than its initial or expected value because of unusual circumstances (such as lack of control, or it is not readily saleable).

**Value**  The worth attached to something exchanged. For purposes of making a gift of LLC interest or corporation stock, for example, you must determine the value of the interest or stock given away. For tax purposes, the fair market value is the value to use.

**Will**  A legal document that contains instructions for the disposal of a person's property under its prescribed terms on said person's death.

**Will contest**  Litigation to overturn a decedent's will for lack of testamentary capacity, undue influence, or lack of proper execution.

# Index

BASE (blending and strategizing
entities) technique
(*continued*)
blending entities, 93–98
intellectual property, 95–96
money makers versus money
losers, 97–98
real estate, 93–94
tools, 96–97
Beneficiaries, 130
Blending entities, 93–98
business tools, 96–97
case study, 189–190
intellectual property, 95–96
keeping real estate separate,
93–94
money makers versus money
losers, 97–98
Business entities. *See also*
Blending entities;
comparison chart, 213–214
defined, 73
and home ownership, 89–91
lack of, 201
personal property owned by, 92
types, 51
Business interruption coverage, 86
Business ownership as tax
shelter, 36–49
fiscal year selection, 46
income shifting, 41–42
incorporating children into
business, 40–41
overview, 36–37

real estate, 42–45
retirement plans, 38–40
Section 179 depreciation,
47–48
tax-free fringe benefits,
37–38
year-end planning, 46–47
Business structure tax and asset
protection comparison
chart, 213–214
Business tools, 96–97

# C

Capital gains, 15, 28, 43, 176
Case studies, 180–190
asset protection, 180–183
blending multiple properties,
189–190
fringe benefits, 183–186
real estate investment, 186–188
Cash basis taxpayers, 46–47
Cash charitable contributions,
26–27
Casualty losses, 29
C corporations:
overview, 51
ownership, asset protection,
taxation, 214
rental income, 56
retail businesses, 53
tax-free fringe benefits,
37–38
as taxpayer type, 19

CD early withdrawal penalty, 25
Certified public accountants
   (CPAs), 126, 196
Charging orders, 98–101
   corporations, 100–101
   limited liability
      companies, 100
   limited partnerships, 99–100
Charitable contributions, 26–27,
   28
Charitable remainder trusts,
   131–132
Child and dependent care tax
   credit, 32
Children, incorporating into
   your business, 40–41
Child tax credit, 32
Clothing, donating to charity, 27
Collectibles, 157
Compounding growth, 7–8,
   138–141
Constructive fraud, 109
Contingency fee lawsuits, 64
Corporate formation, 103
Corporate maintenance,
   103–105
Corporations. *See also* C corpo-
   rations; S corporations
   and charging orders,
      100–101
   deductions checklist,
      207–208
   defined, 77
   overview, 77–78

stock market wealth
   structuring, 174
Cost segregation, 45
CPAs (certified public
   accountants), 126, 196
Cyberspace policy, 86

# D

Data policy, 86
Death taxes. *See* Estate taxes
Debt strategy, 91–93, 159–161
Deductions:
   above-the-line, 22–25
   casualty losses, 29
   charitable contributions,
      26–27, 28
   checklist, 207–211
   education, military,
      government, 22–23
   general, 207–208
   gifts of appreciated
      property, 28
   health, 23–24
   investment interest paid, 28
   for investors, 172
   itemized, 25–30
   medical expenses, 26,
      208–211
   miscellaneous, 25, 29–30
   mortgage interest, 27
   moving expenses, 24
   points and loan origination
      fees, 27–28

Multiple entity structuring
strategy. *See* Legal MESS
(multiple entity structuring
strategy); Tax MESS
(multiple entity structuring
strategy)
Multiplier effect, 165–166

## N

National Guard members, 23
Nonbusiness energy property
tax credit, 33
Nonqualified retirement plans,
152–153

## O

Operating agreement, 81
Other people's money (OPM),
165–166, 175

## P

Partnerships. *See* General
partnerships; Limited
partnerships
Passive income, 15
Pass-through taxation, 76, 176
Pension plans. *See also* Retirement plans
asset protection benefits,
155–156

bankruptcy exemptions by
state, 215–227
money purchase, 150
Pension Protection Act of 2006,
143–144
Performing artists, 25
Personal property owned by
business, 92
Personal representatives,
124–126
Personal tax deductions, 21–31,
32–33
above-the-line, 22–25
itemized, 25–30
tax credits, 30–31, 32–33
Piercing the corporate veil,
105–107
Planning, estate. *See* Estate
planning
Planning, year-end, 46–47
Points and loan origination fees,
27–28
Portfolio income, 15
Post-judgment exemptions by
state, 215–227
Pour-over wills, 135
Probate, 124–127
and life insurance, 129
procedures, 125–127
and revocable living trust,
130
Prohibited transaction rules, for
IRAs, 161–164
Property policies, 84

Trusts:
  charitable remainder, 131–132
  as estate planning tool, 130–132
  irrevocable life insurance, 132
  revocable living, 89–91,
    130–131
  spendthrift, 132
Tuition and fees deduction, 23,
    199–201

## U

Umbrella policies, 86
Uniform Fraudulent Convey-
  ance Act (UFCA), 108
Uniform Fraudulent Transfer
  Act (UFTA), 108–109

Unrelated business taxable
  income (UBIT), 159–161
Valuation discounts, 134

## W

W-2 wages, 15
Wealth protection. *See* Asset
  protection
Wills, 129, 135
Working during retirement,
    144–145

## Y

Year-end planning, 46–47

# 90% of Americans Retire Broke.

## Wealth is a Choice. What Do You Choose?

20% of the population owns 80% of the world's wealth. To belong to this 20% is your choice. You can choose to struggle to make ends meet, or you can choose to experience the freedom of living your life the way you want.

The difference between the two is… **active effort** and the **right direction.**

**The Wealth Builder Action Plan gives you this right direction.**

**8** Programs in all, each presented by a different world-class expert.

**4** Take you down four distinct pathways to wealth.

**3** Establish action-orientated fundamentals that position you to win.

**1** Tells you how to protect the wealth you create.

**The Road to Wealth is a Choice, But Only if You Take These Steps.**

Log on to www.TrumpUniversity.com/ActionPlan or call 1-877-508-7867 to order your copy of The Wealth Builder's Action Plan Today!

TRUMP UNIVERSITY

# Get Your FREE Special Report from Donald J. Trump!

Perhaps you know who I am… if so, then you know that I know a thing or two about real estate — and now I'm ready to teach you! Frankly, I think everyone can achieve their financial dreams and enjoy a more luxurious life by mastering the "art of the deal" — you just have to learn how.

## What Makes Real Estate the World's Best Investment?

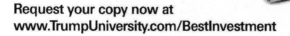

FREE Special Report

**Request your copy now at
www.TrumpUniversity.com/BestInvestment**

The report won't cost you a penny — but it really could help you develop the skills and perspective you need to succeed beyond your wildest dreams. Better yet, it will introduce you to Trump University — a world-class lineup of personal coaching, online courses, live teleseminars, and home study programs designed to give you a huge advantage in your life!

No opportunity lasts forever — so do it now.

## TRUMP
### UNIVERSITY

www.TrumpUniversity.com

## PERSONAL GOALS:

- ☑ Get promoted.
- ☑ Fire my boss.
- ☑ Start my own business.
- ☑ Buy a home.
- ☑ Flip a home.
- ☑ Enjoy financial independence.
- ☑ Live larger.
- ☑ Laugh more.
- ☑ Achieve my dreams.

## START RIGHT HERE:
## www.TrumpUniversity.com

Donald J. Trump knows about success. He lives it. He epitomizes it. And now he's ready to *teach* it — with world-class instructors, convenient online learning programs, and a wealth of streetwise wealth-building wisdom that can give you a lifelong professional and personal advantage.

Visit our website today — **www.TrumpUniversity.com** to learn more, do more, and BE more. The information is absolutely free — but the opportunity could be priceless.

www.TrumpUniversity.com

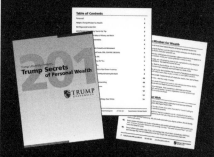